D. S. Publishers (India)
the Bookmaster
DELHI

Language Skills

Pre-Primary Learning Skills
B
Crayon

Pre-Writing Skills

Shab

This book belongs to

____

____

D. S. Publishers (India)

First Published 2001
15th Impression 2018

ISBN 9788187131632

Published by
DS Publishers India
4325/3 Ansari Road, Daryaganj
New Delhi 110002, INDIA
info@dspublishers.com
www.dspublishers.com

Typesetting and Cover Design by
Lovika Arts

Printed in India at
Balaji Offset

PREFACE

Children of the ages between 3 years and 5 years are at the Pre-Primary stage of learning, and just about awakened to their sensory skills.

This series of books is basically revolving round children of these ages — and are thus directed towards the development of the skills to which the tiny beings are getting introduced to. They are being initiated into the concepts that are necessary for further progress of the learning procedures.

This set of books deals separately with specific language skills. With these books at hand, followed by the guidance of the teacher or parents will take the children ahead in fixing in their minds the correct concepts necessary for further education.

The activities enshrined in these books help the child in developing his/her basic skills of reading and writing.

Eye-hand Co-ordination Top to Bottom

Join the dots.

Teacher/Parents : Encourage the child to draw from top to bottom.

Horizontal and Vertical Strokes

Draw Father Mouse straps.

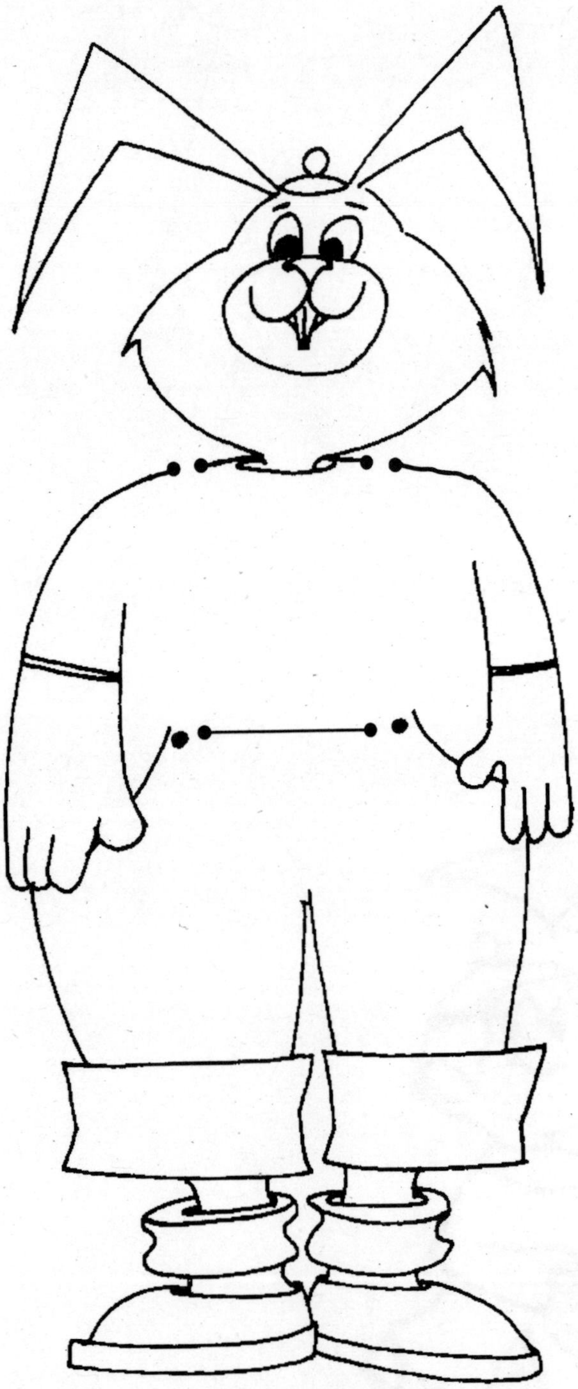

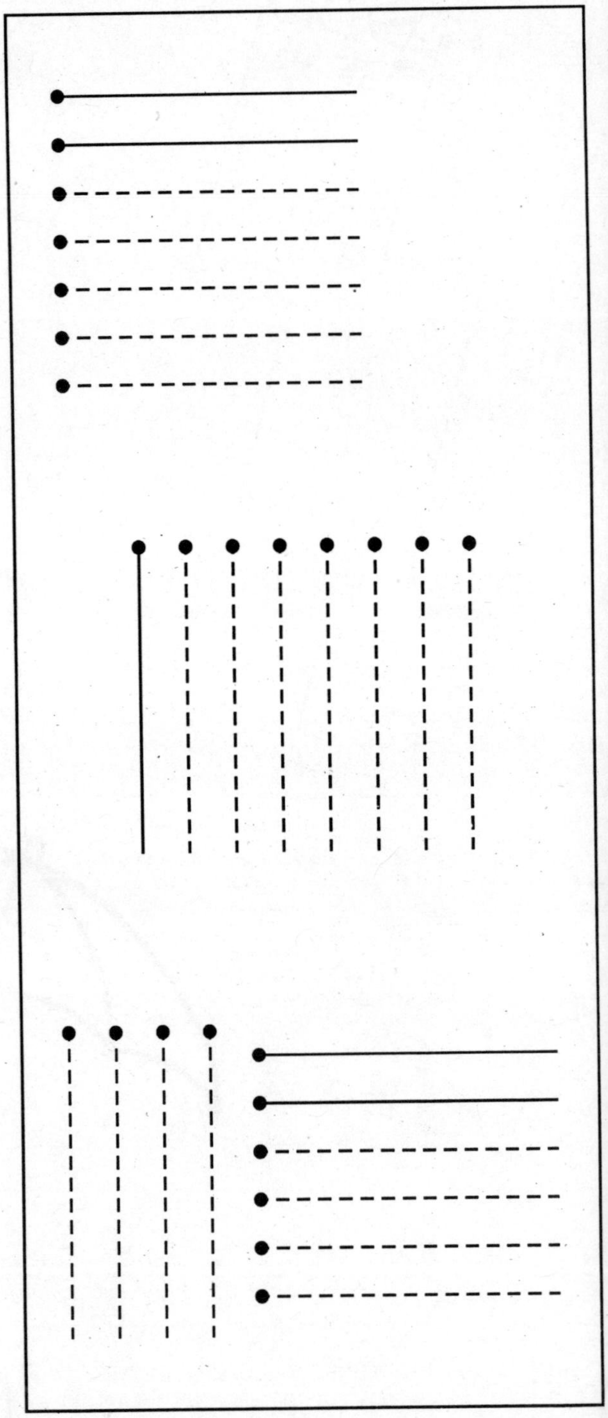

Teacher/Parents : Direct the child to complete the horizontal and vertical patterns.

Left-Right and Up-Down Strokes

Where the Ants are going?

Teacher/Parents : Further practice for straight, left-right and up-down strokes.

Eye-Hand Co-ordination — Oblique Strokes

Trace the dots to join the pictures.

Teacher/Parents : Discuss the pictures with the child and ask him/her to draw more oblique strokes.

Left to Right and Right to Left Oblique Strokes

Trace the dots to form a tree.

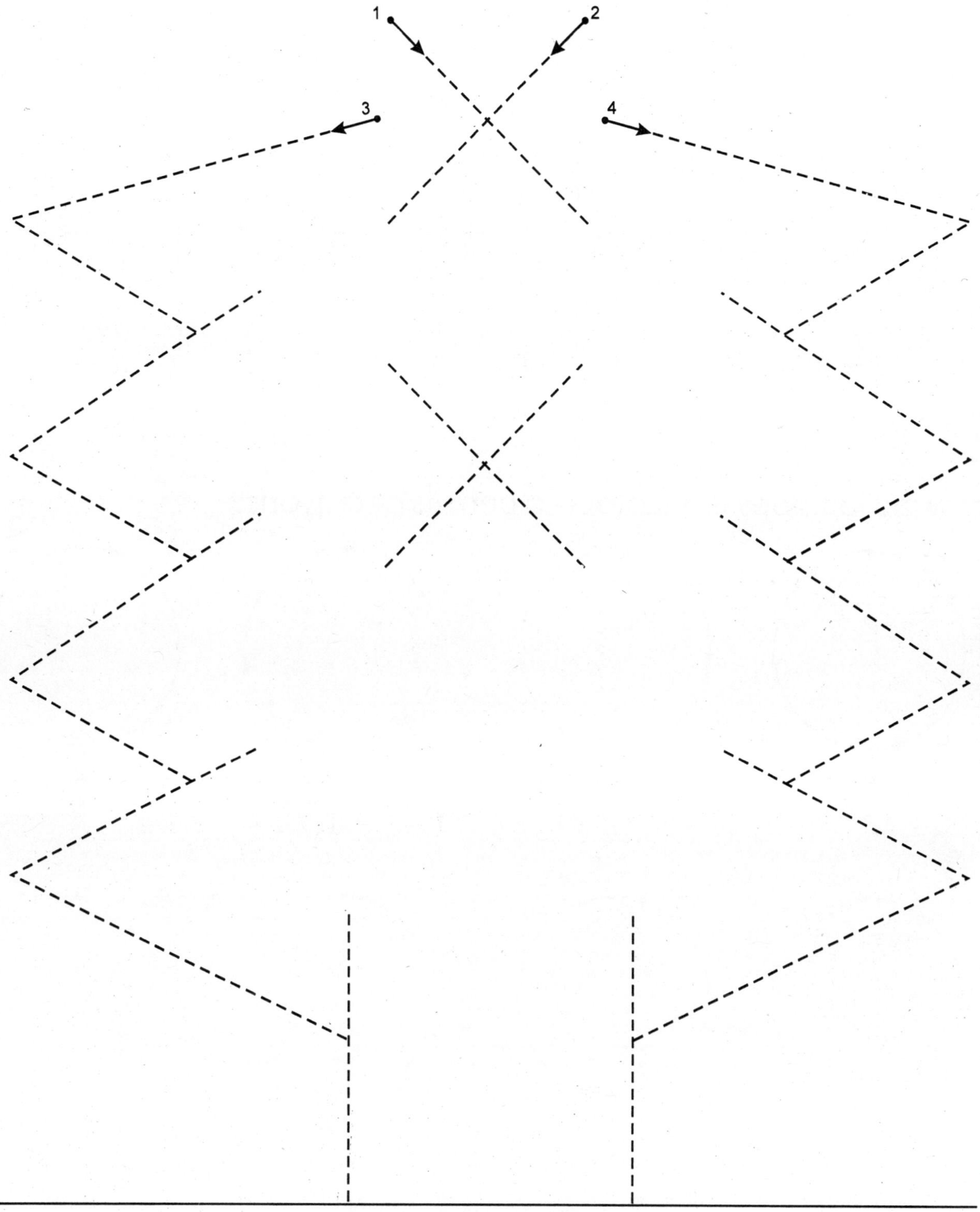

Teacher/Parents : Ask the child to begin with the left to right stroke, follow by the right to left strokes.

Circular Strokes

Trace the circles using crayons or coloured pencils.

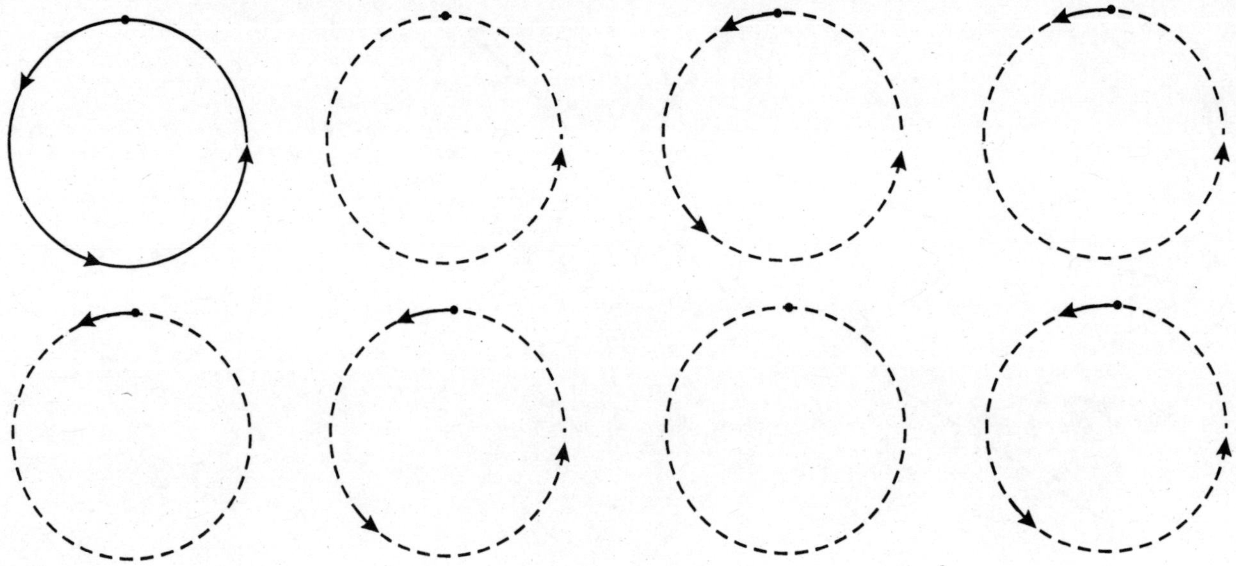

Draw the lollipops with coloured pencils or crayons.

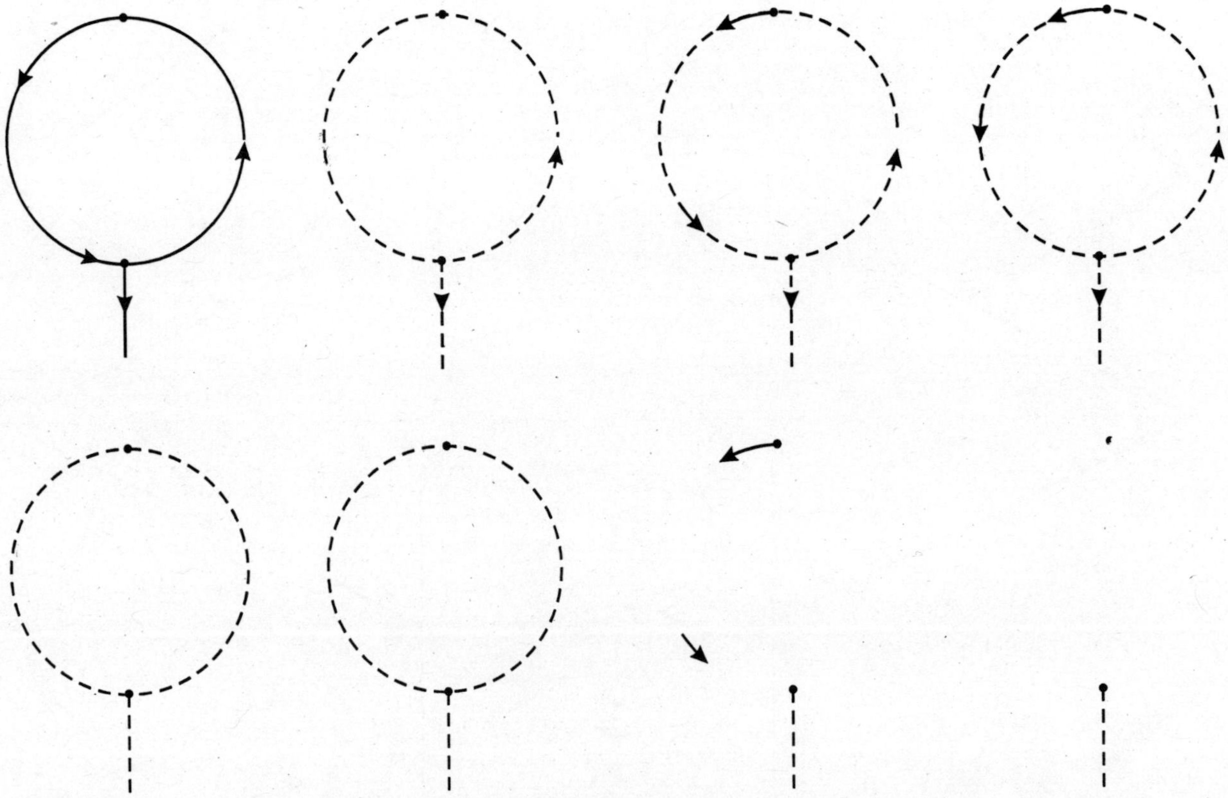

Teacher/Parents : Direct the child to draw circles in an anti-clockwise direction.

Circular Strokes

Use coloured pencils or crayons to trace the bubbles.

Teacher/Parents : More practice on correct formation of circular stroke.

Over-swing Strokes

Trace the dotted lines.

Teacher/Parents : Direct the child to concentrate on eye-hand co-ordination for over-swing pattern.

Under-swing Strokes

Trace the dotted lines.

Teacher/Parents : Direct the child to concentrate on eye-hand co-ordination for under-swing pattern.

Over-swing and Under-swing Strokes

Trace the dotted lines to help the animals get their food.

Teacher/Parents : Children must begin eye-hand movement from left to right in reading and writing.

Over-swing and Under-swing Patterns

Trace the over-swing and under-swing patterns.

Teacher/Parents : Direct the child to complete the patterns for correct formation of b, e, and p.

Over-swing Strokes for Letters m,n

Let us make patterns.

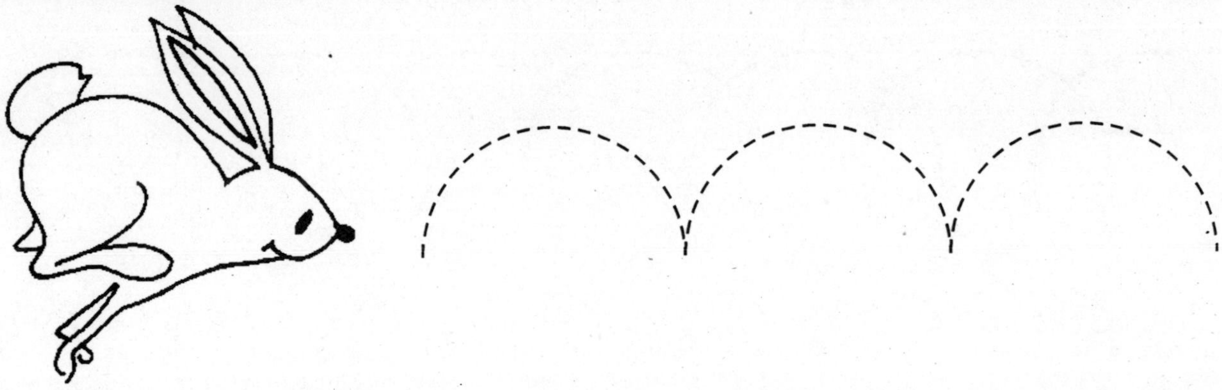

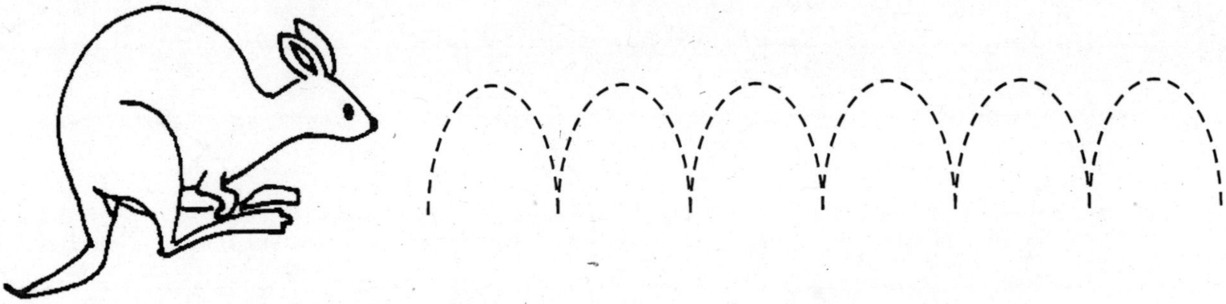

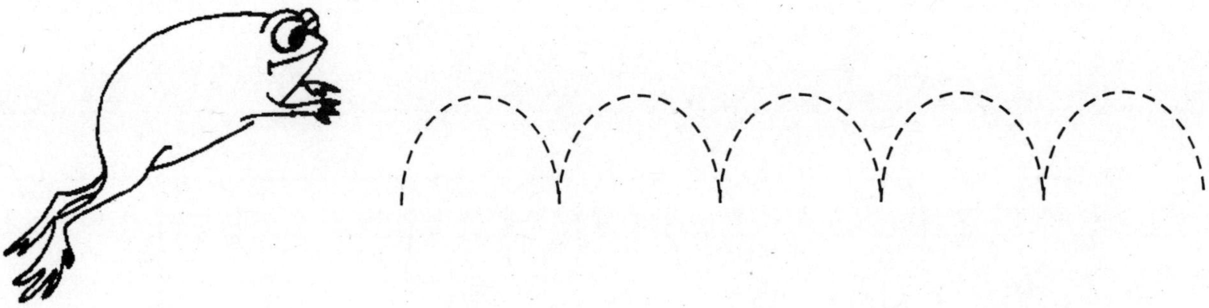

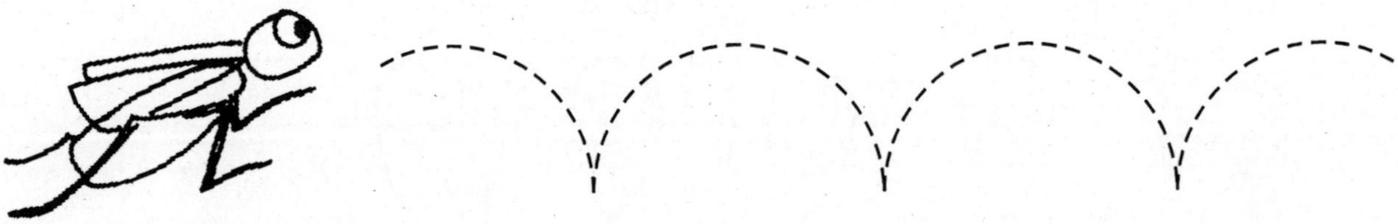

Teacher/Parents : Direct the child about over-swing pattern for formation of letters m, n. Ask him/her to help the rabbit, the grasshopper, the frog and the kangaroo find their way home.

Eye-Hand Co-ordination

Trace the flowers.

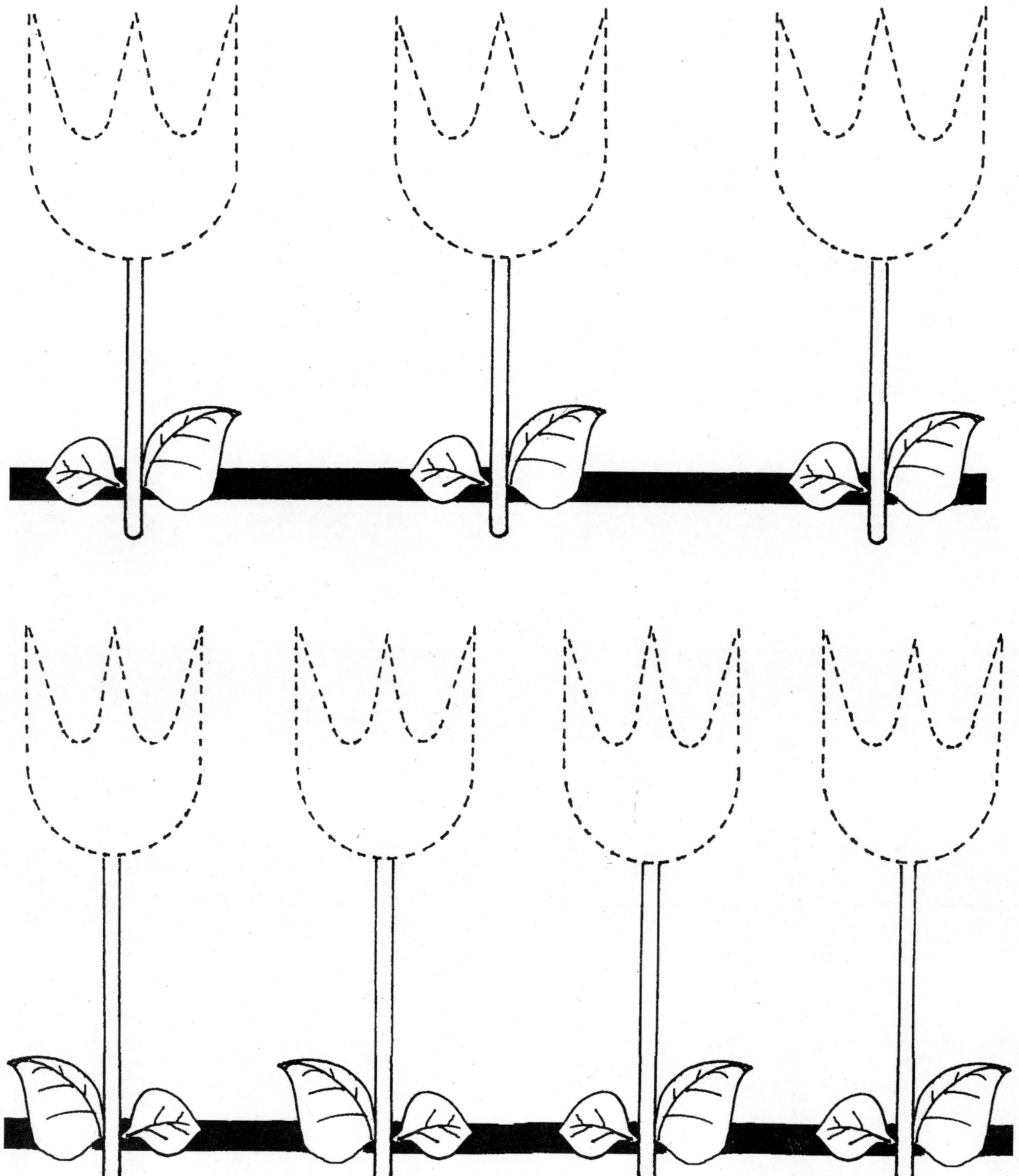

Teacher/Parents : Direct the child about under-swing strokes for letter 'u'.

Over-swing and Under-swing Patterns

Trace the patterns.

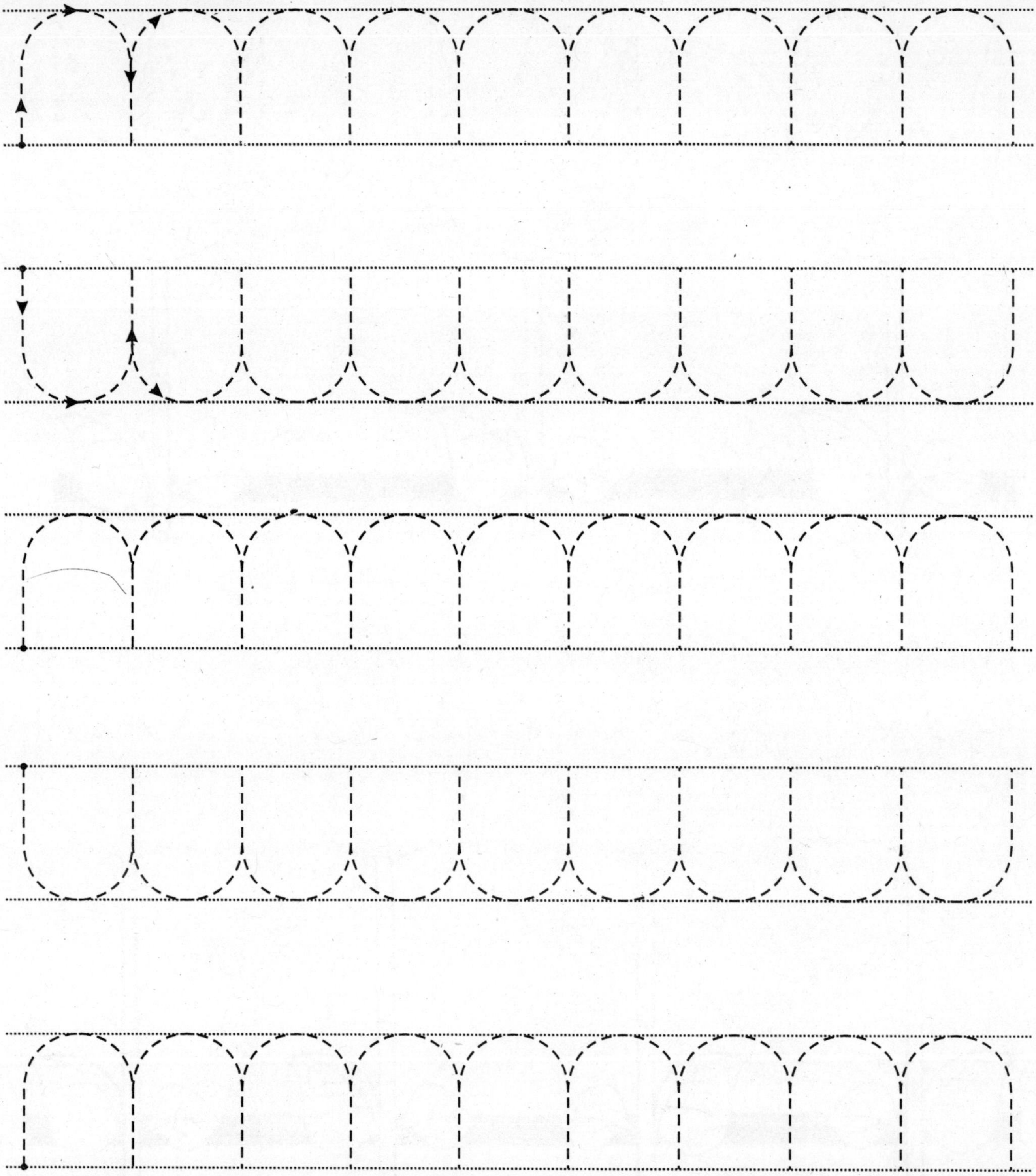

Teacher/Parents : Help the child in understanding over-swing and under-swing patterns for correct formation of letters 'n' and 'u'.

Formation of Letters 's'

Join the dots to complete the pictures.

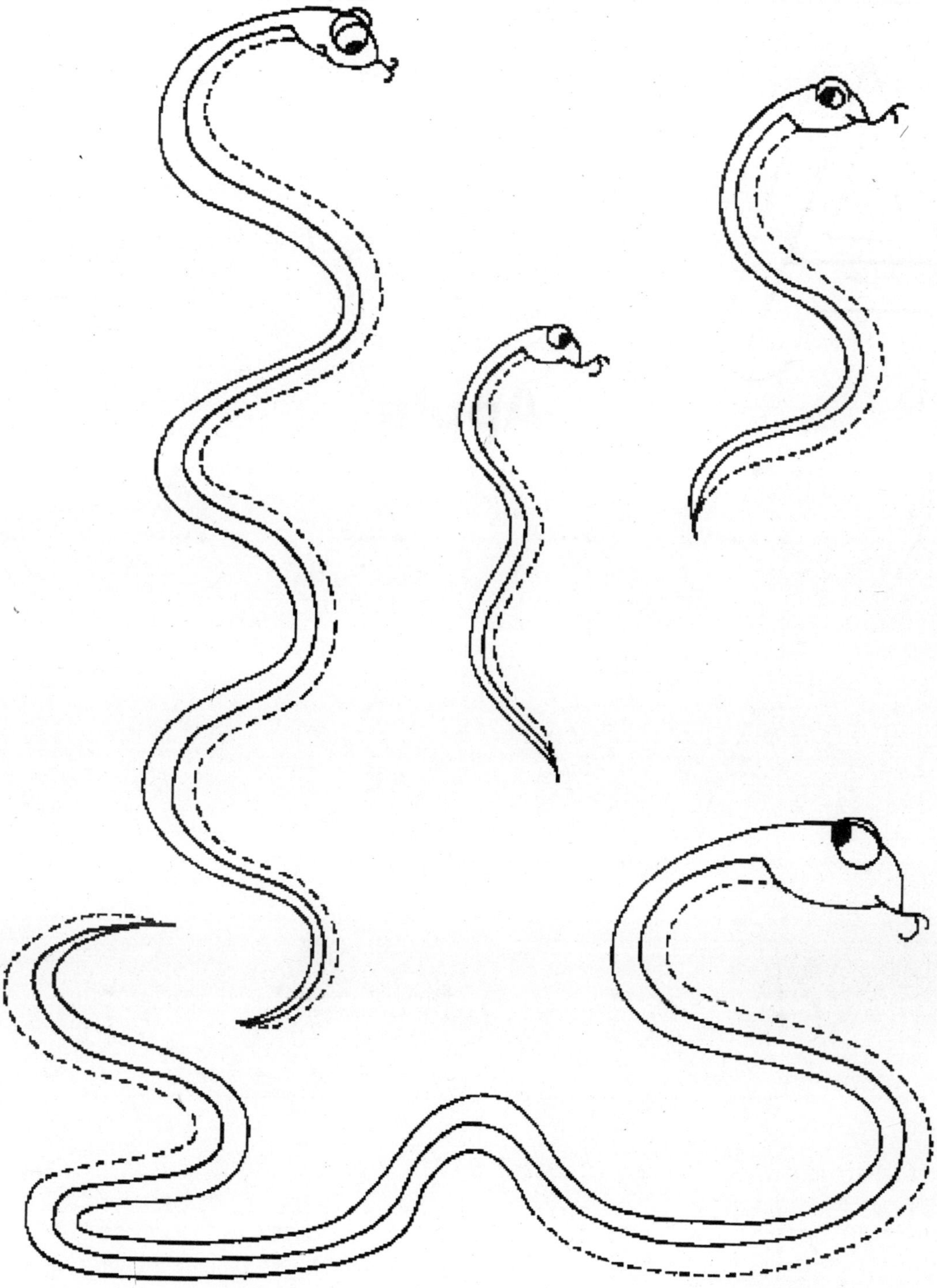

Teacher/Parents : Eye-hand co-ordination for letter 's'. Allow practice on large sheets of paper.

Read and Write - Alphabet

Trace the letter **A a**.

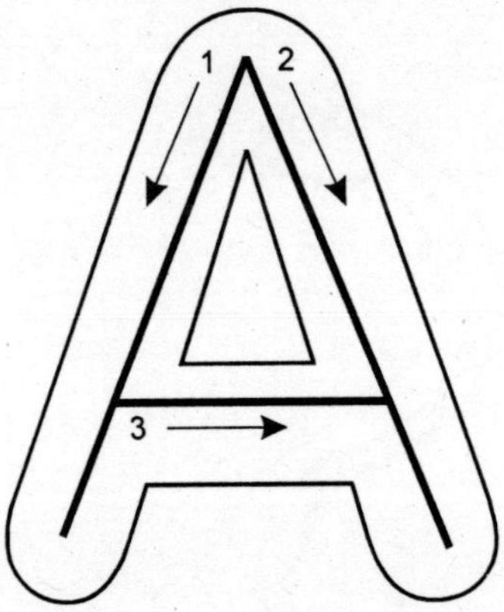

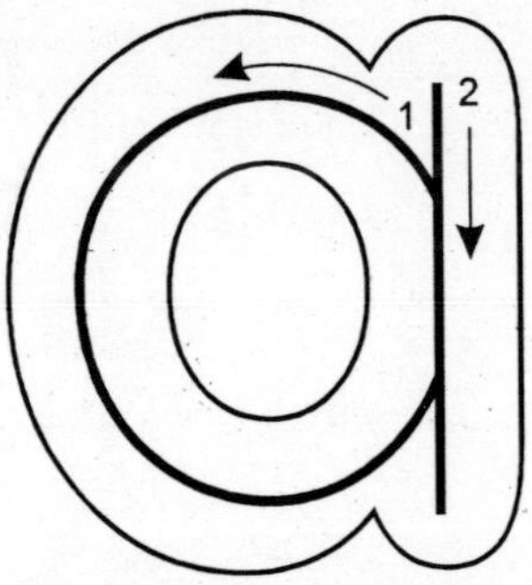

Apple

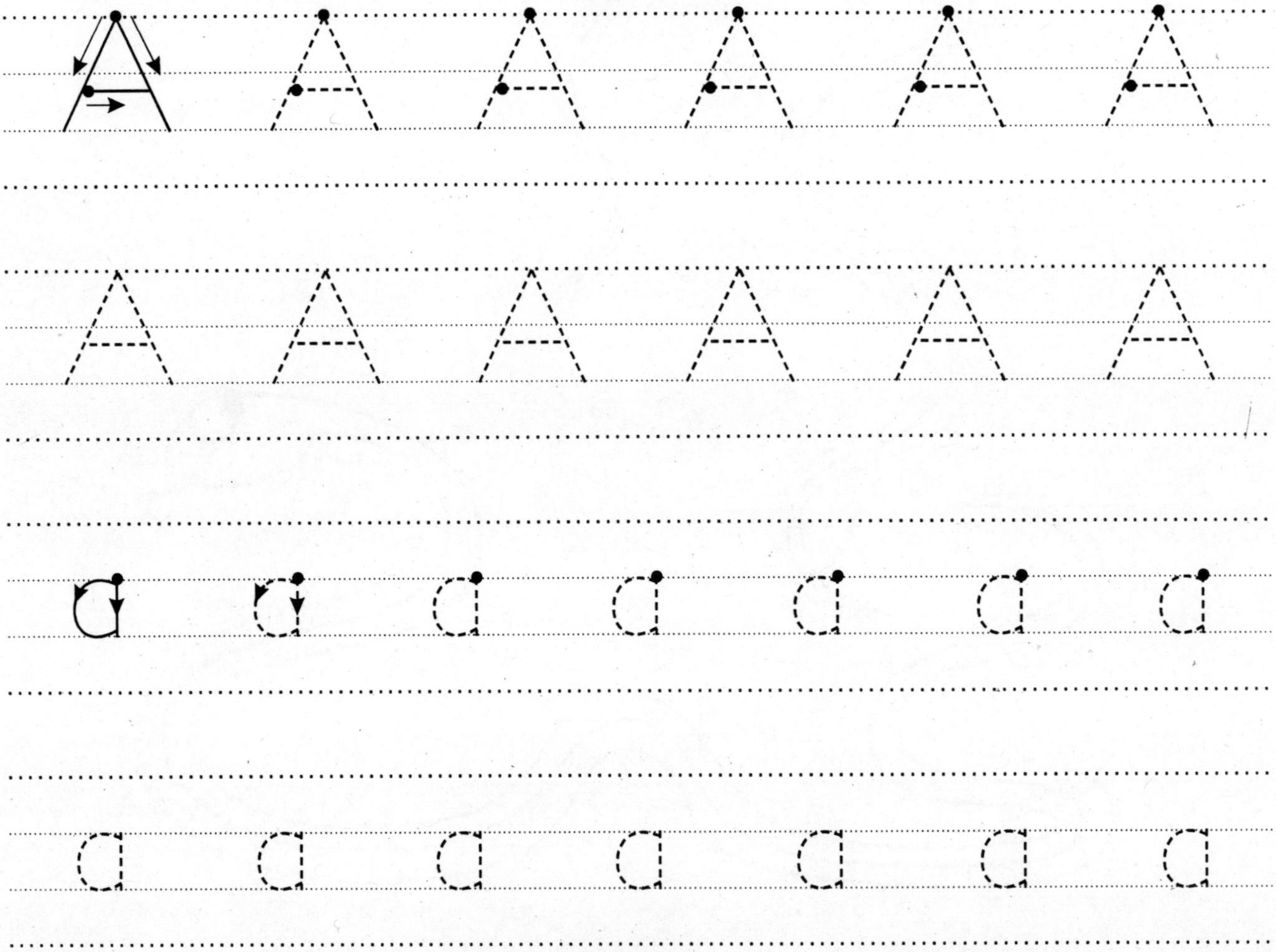

Teacher/Parents : Ask the child to read and identify the letter.

A A A A A A

A A A

A

a a a a a a a

a a a

a a

Alphabet

Trace the letter **B b**.

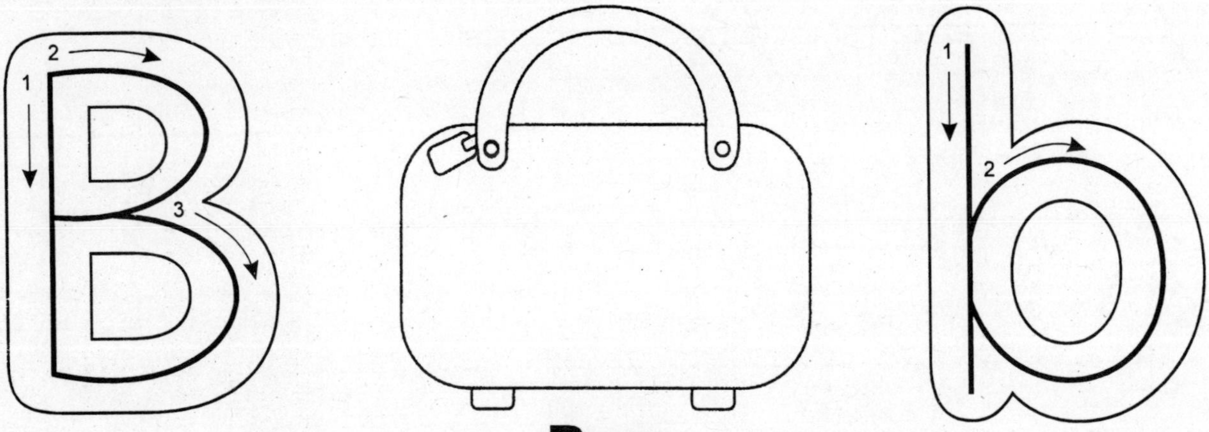

Bag

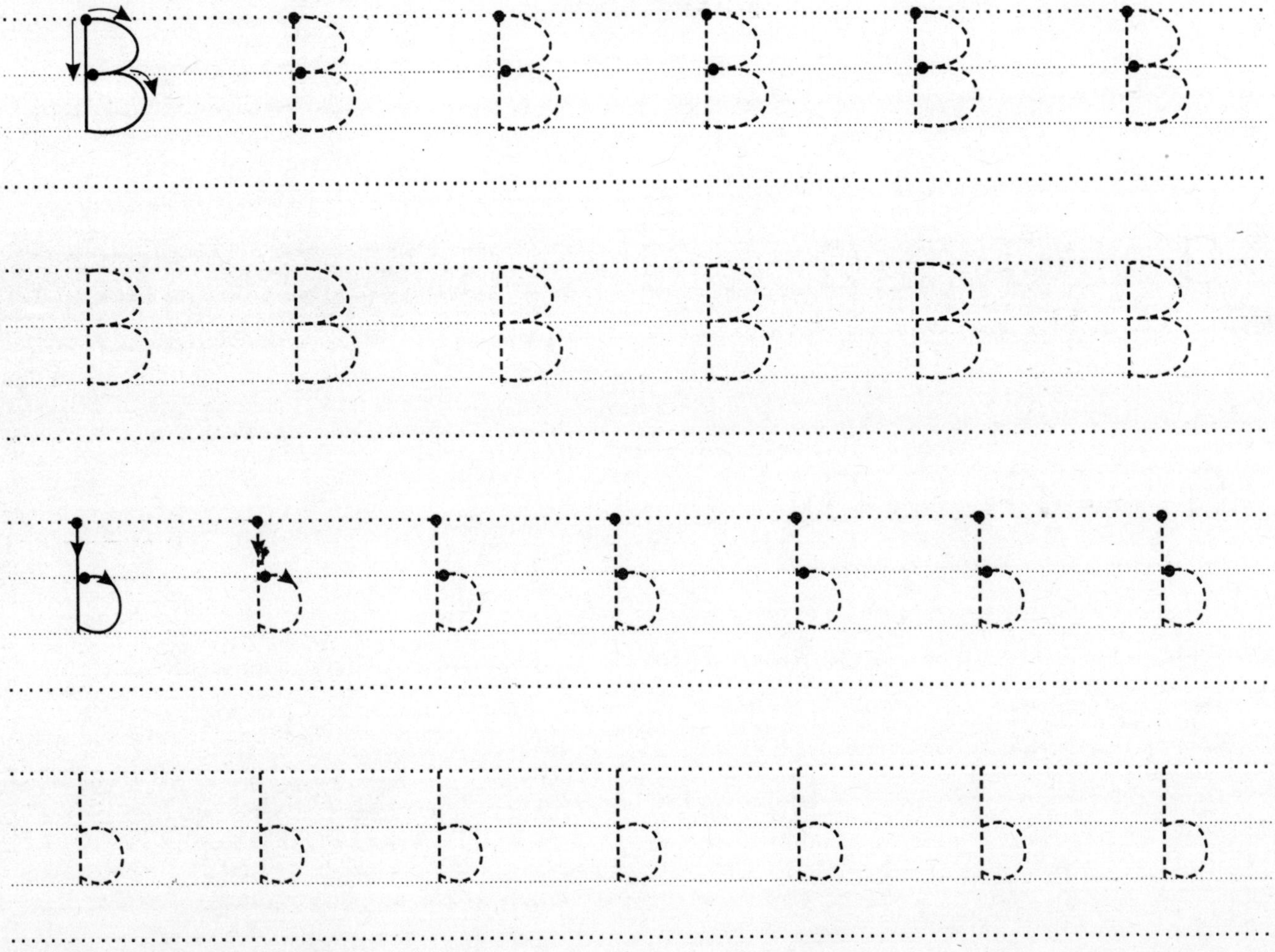

Teacher/Parents : Ask the child to complete the letter shape and identify.

B B B B B B

B B B

B

b b b b b b b

b b b

b b

Trace the letter **C c**.

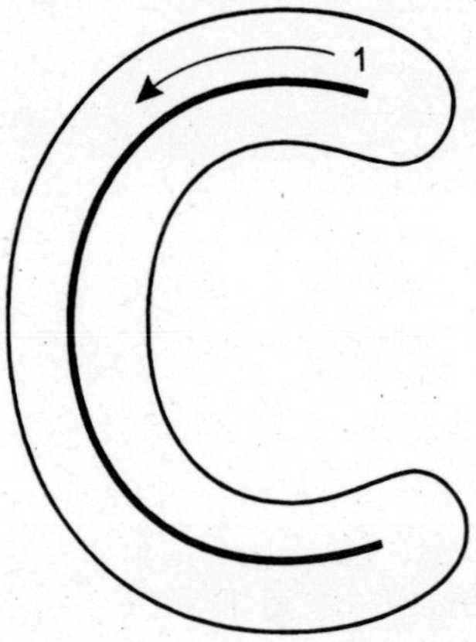

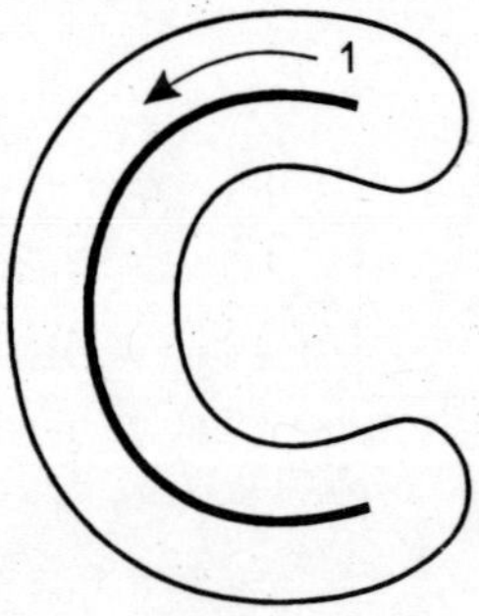

Clown

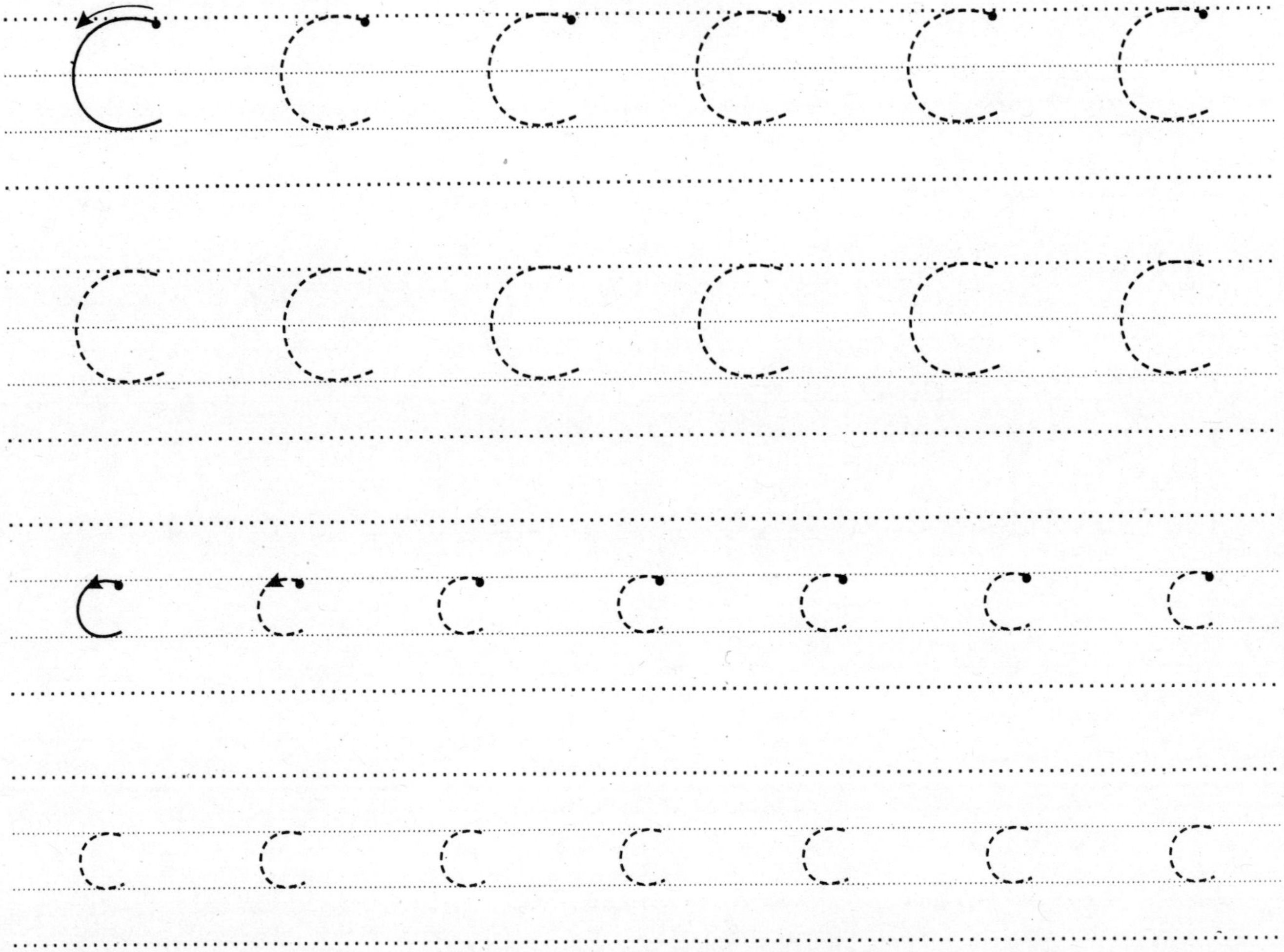

Teacher/Parents : Ask the child to complete the letter and read aloud.

C C C C C C

C C C

C

c c c c c c c

c c c

c c

Trace the letter **D d**.

Donkey

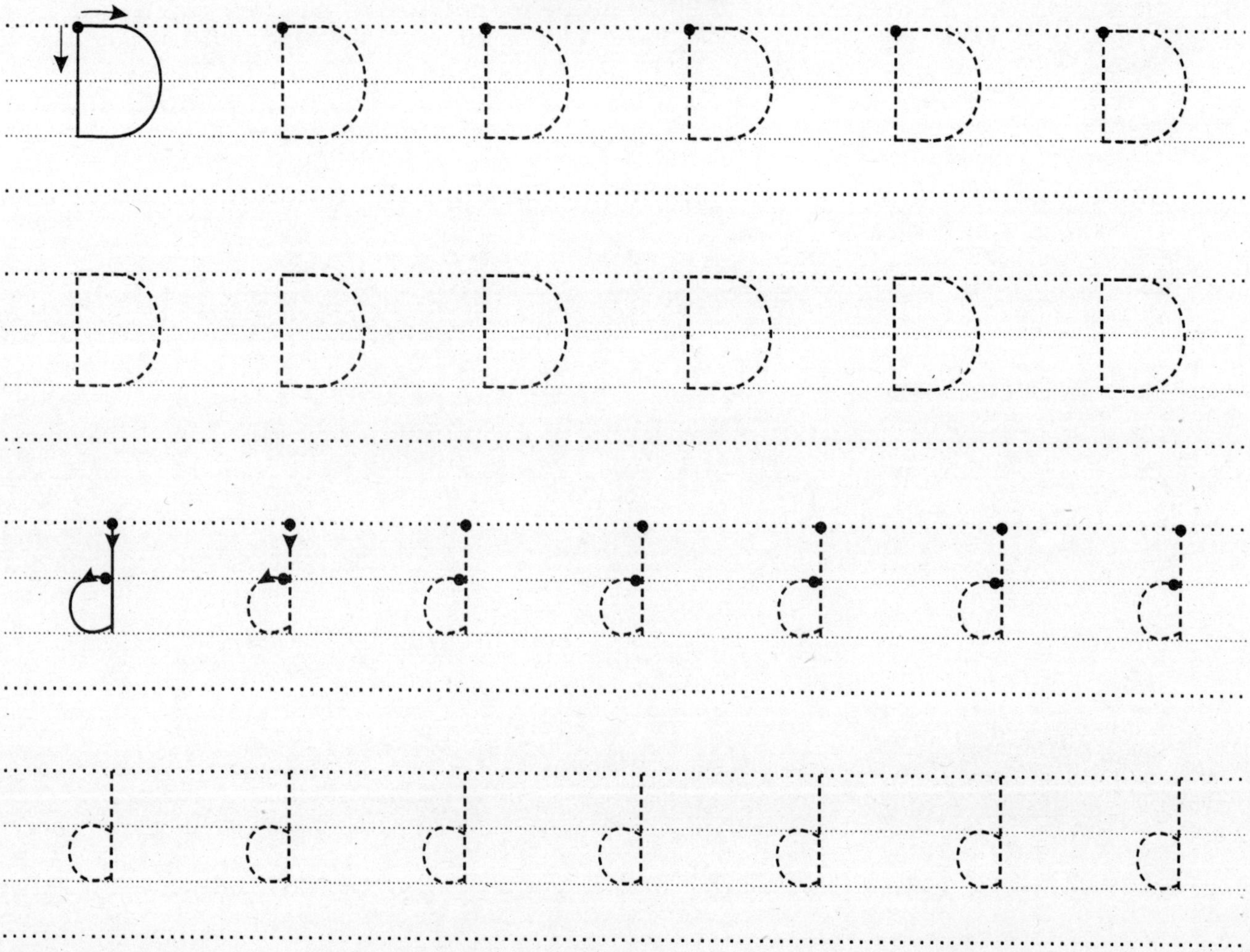

Teacher/Parents : Help the child to complete the letter. Ask him to read aloud and identify.

D D D D D D

D D D

D

d d d d d d d

d d d

d d

Alphabet

Trace the letter **E e**.

Elephant

Teacher/Parents : Help the child to join the dots. Ask him to read aloud and identify the letter.

E E E E E E

E E E

E

e e e e e e e

e e e

e e

Trace the letter **F f**.

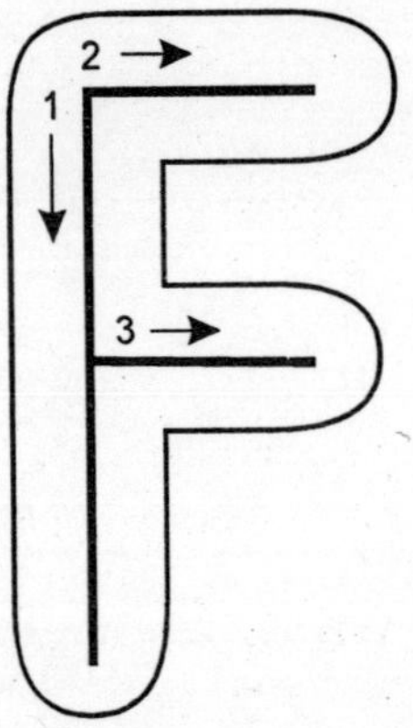

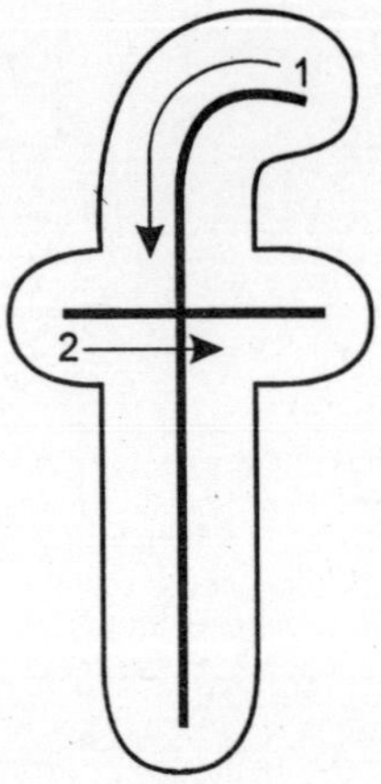

Fox

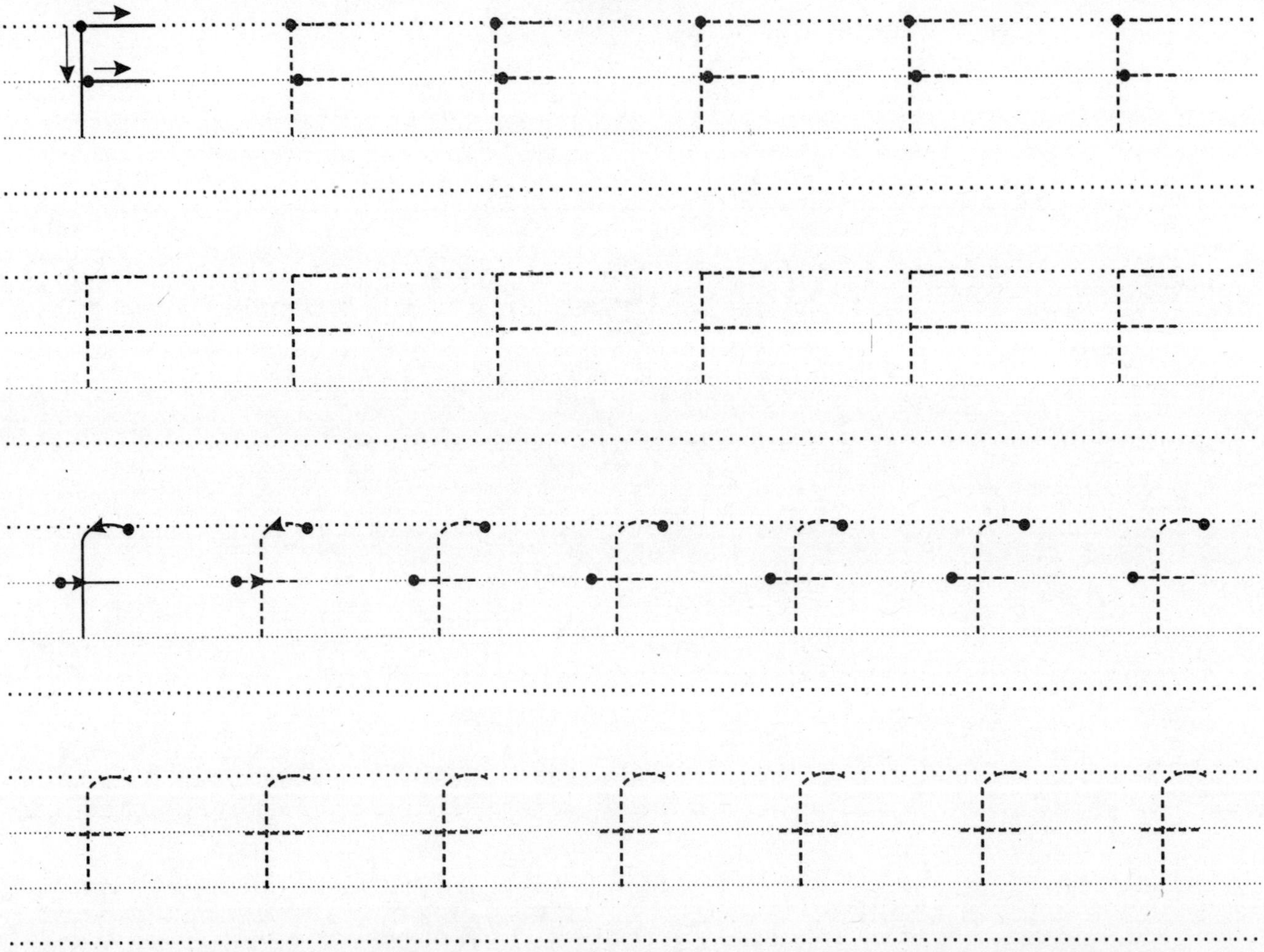

Teacher/Parents : Help the child to complete the letter. Ask him to read aloud and identify.

F F F F F F

F F F

F

f f f f f f f

f f f

f f

Alphabet

Trace the letter **G g**.

Grapes

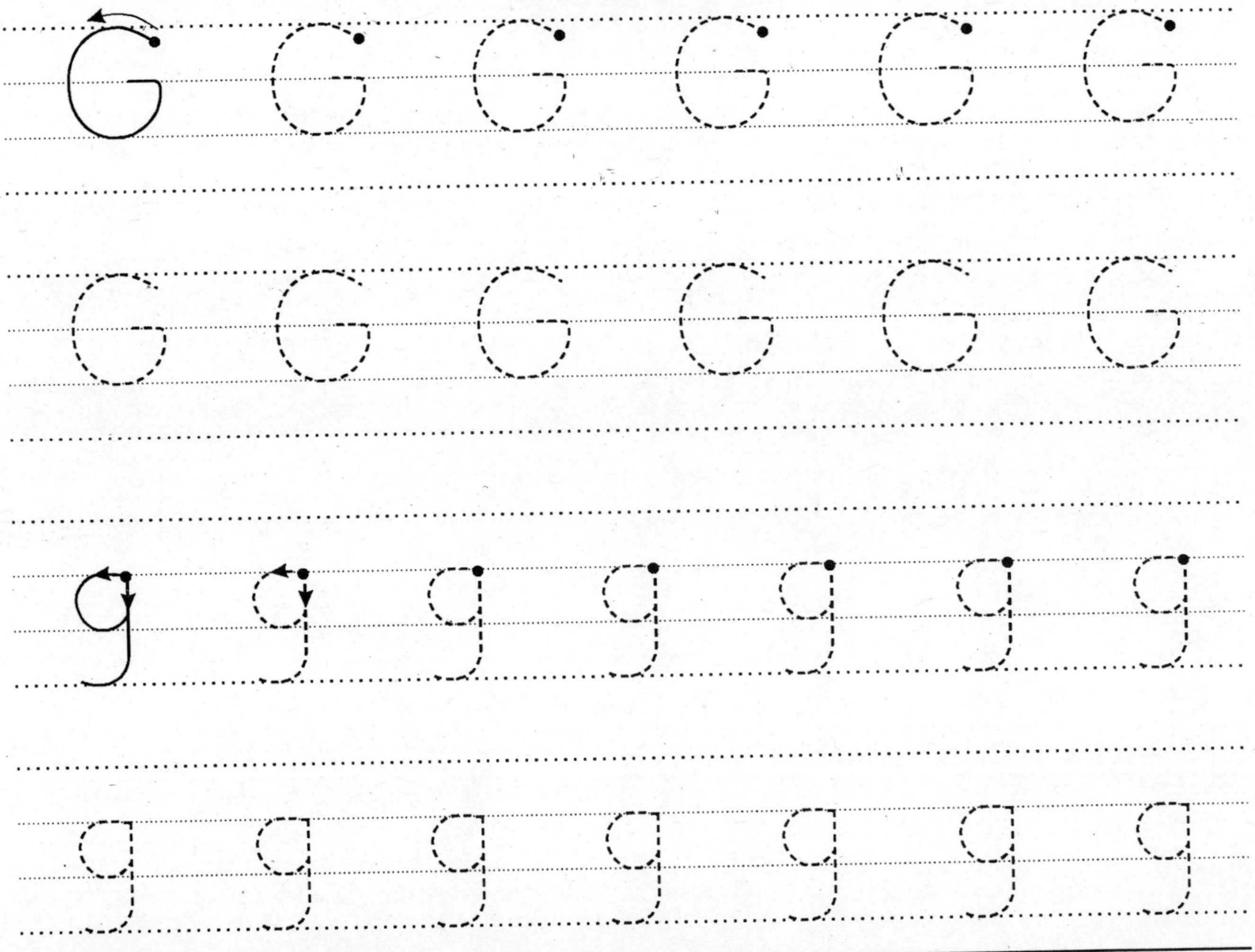

Teacher/Parents : Ask the child to read and identify the letter.

G G G G G G

G G G

G

g g g g g g g

g g g

g g

Trace the letter **H h**.

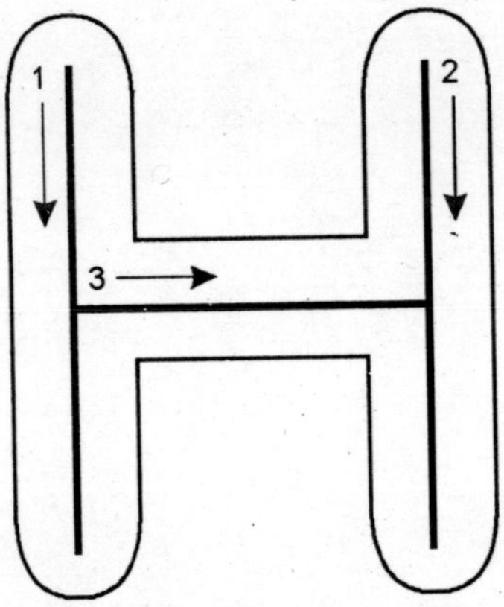

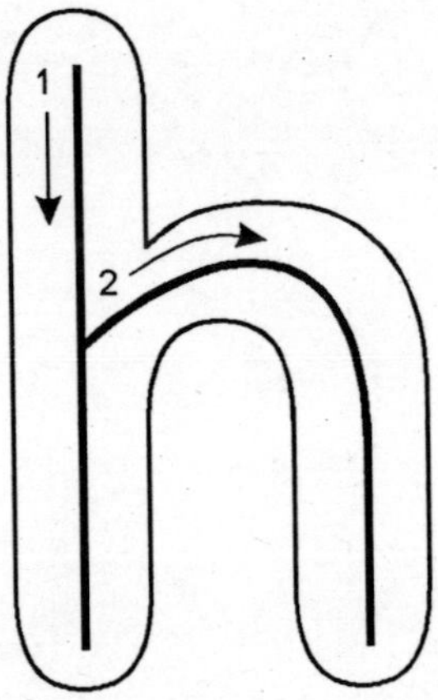

Hen

Teacher/Parents : Ask the child to complete the letter shape and identify.

H H H H H H

H H H

H

h h h h h h h

h h h

h h

Alphabet

Trace the letter **I i**.

Ice

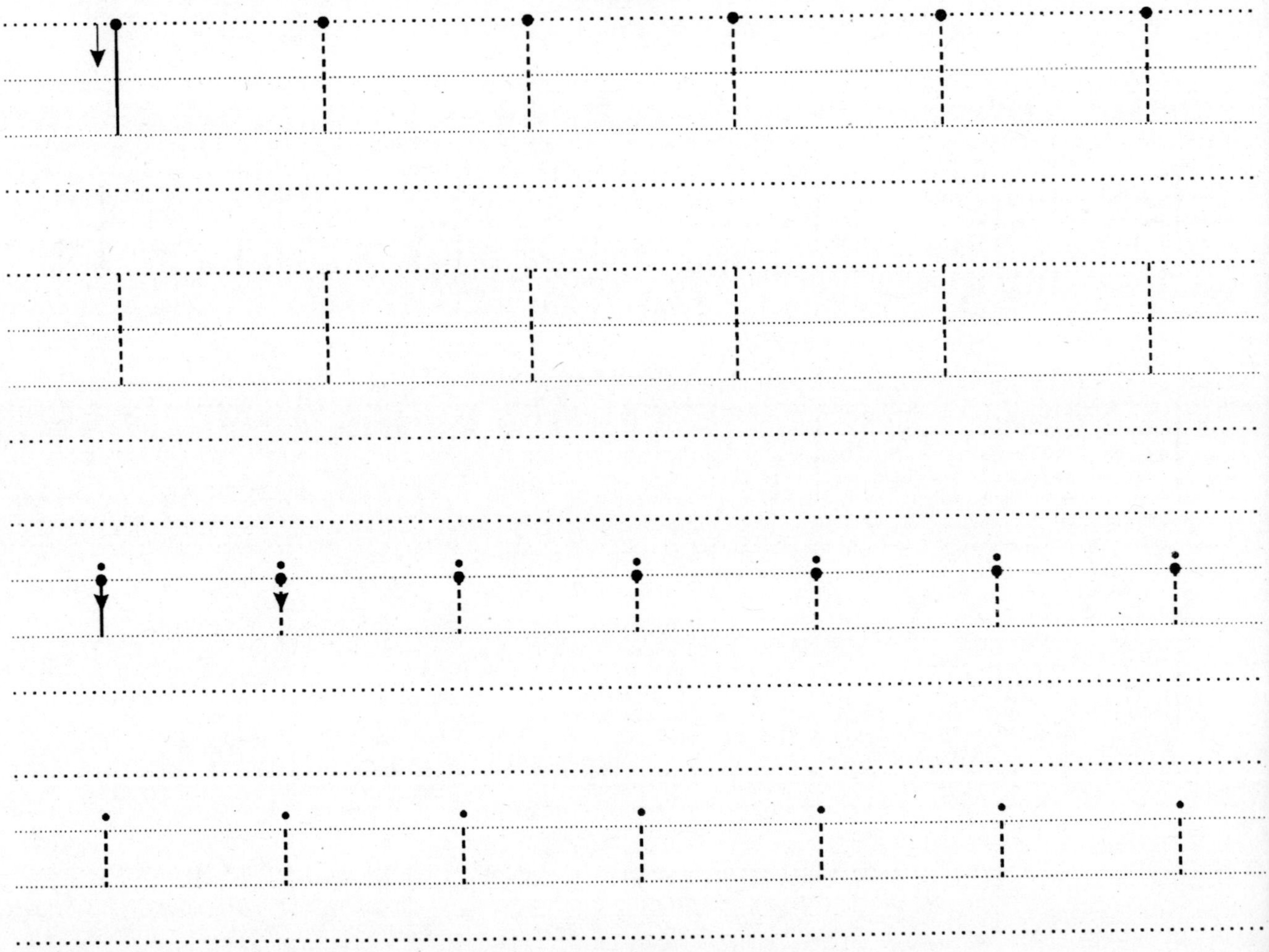

Teacher/Parents : Ask the child to complete the letter and read aloud.

Trace the letter **Jj**.

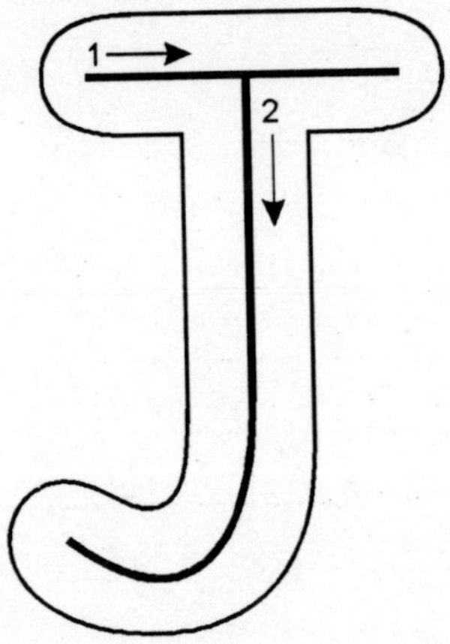

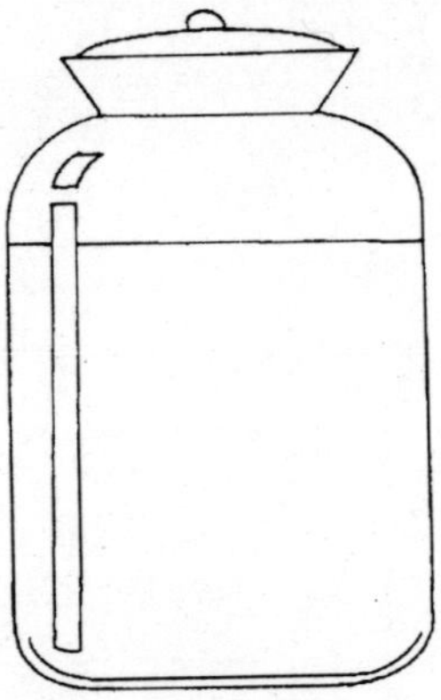

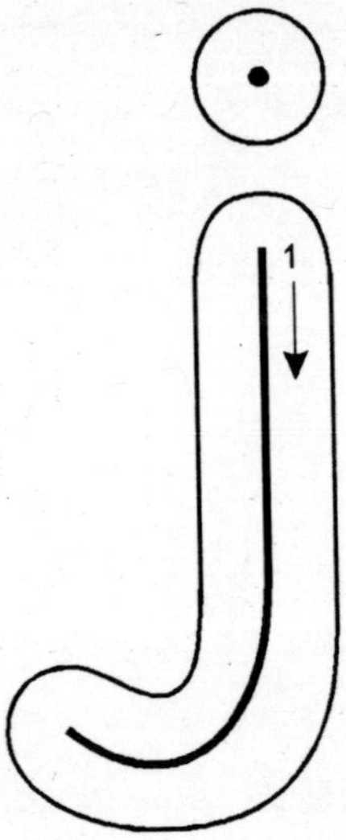

Jar

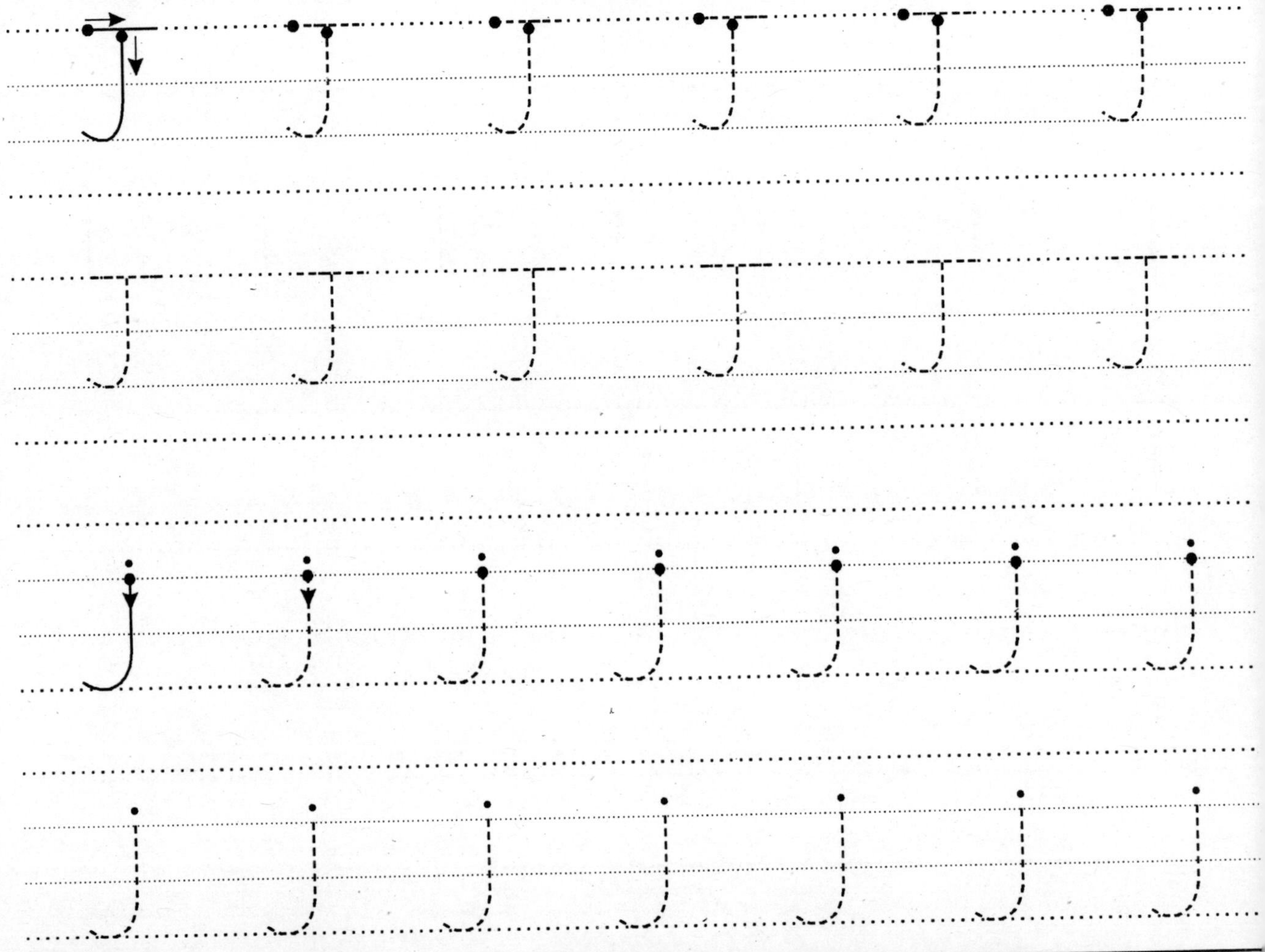

Teacher/Parents : Help the child to complete the letter. Ask him to read aloud and identify.

J J J J J J

J J J

J

j j j j j j j

j j j

j j

Alphabet

Trace the letter **K k**.

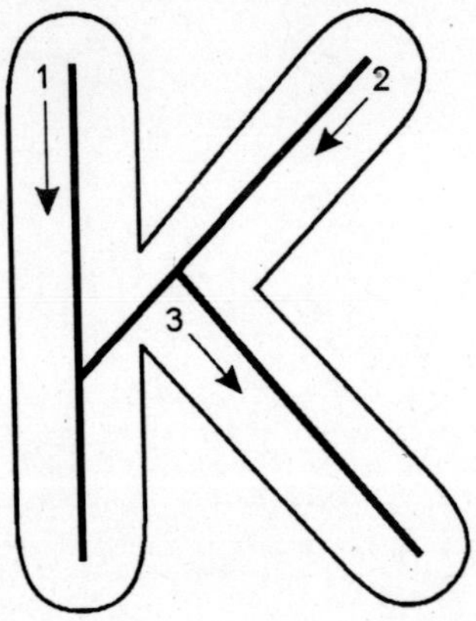

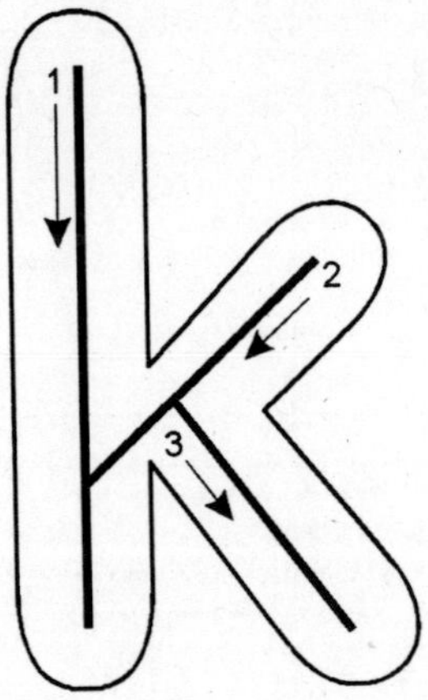

Kangaroo

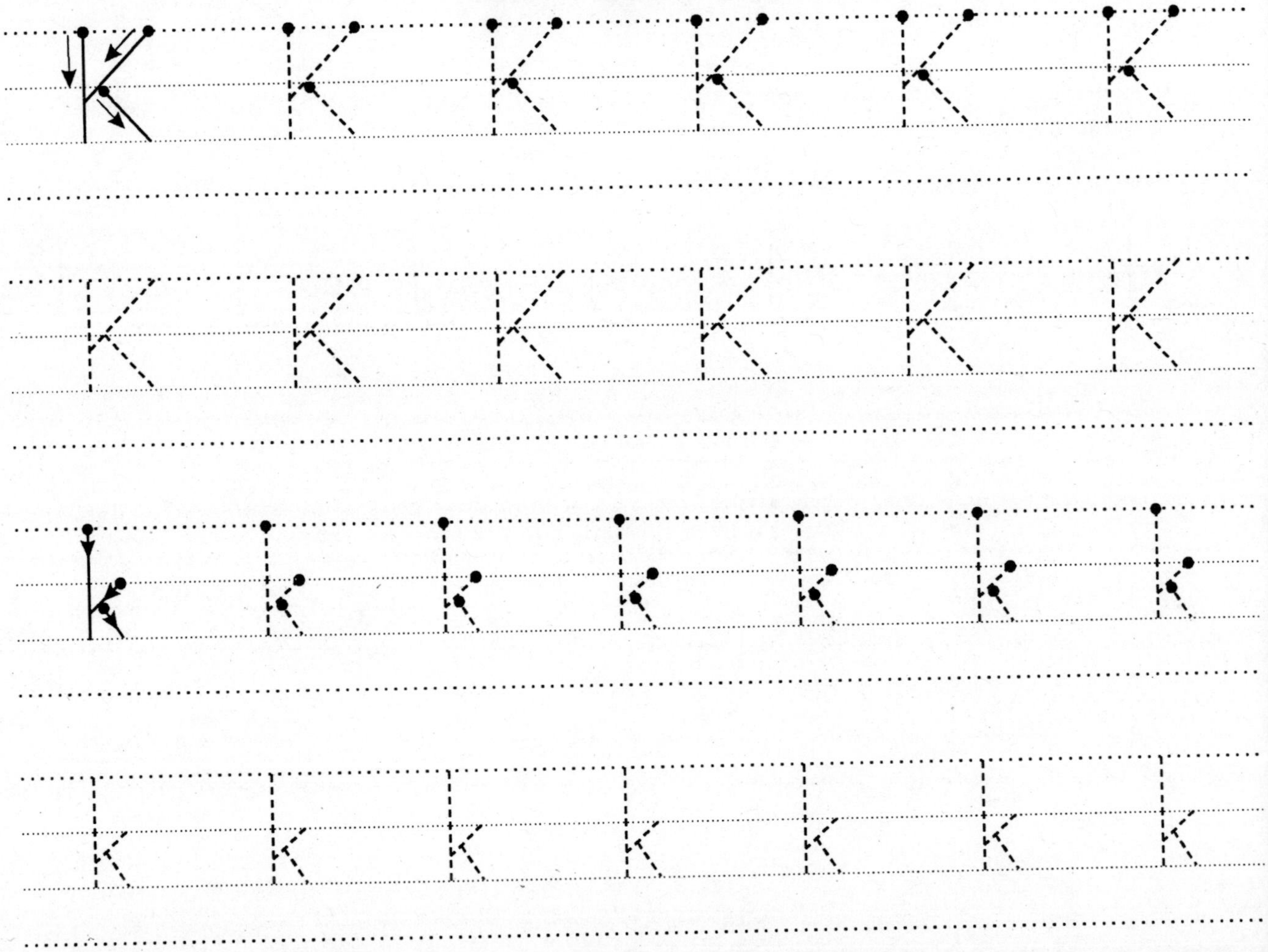

Teacher/Parents : Help the child to join the dots. Ask him to read aloud and identify the letter.

K K K K K K

K K K

K

k k k k k k k

k k k

k k

Trace the letter **L l**.

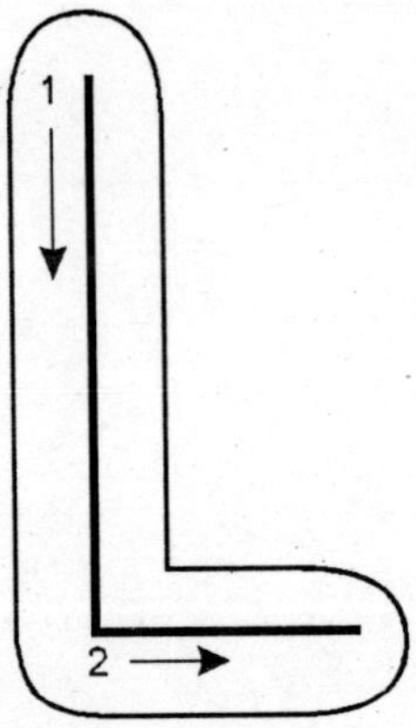

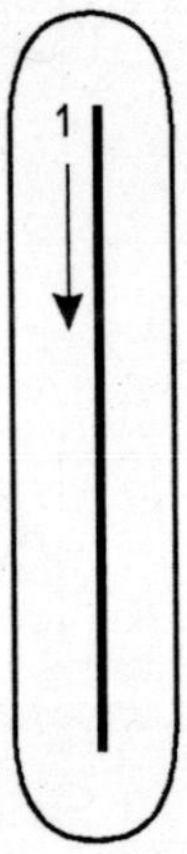

Lion

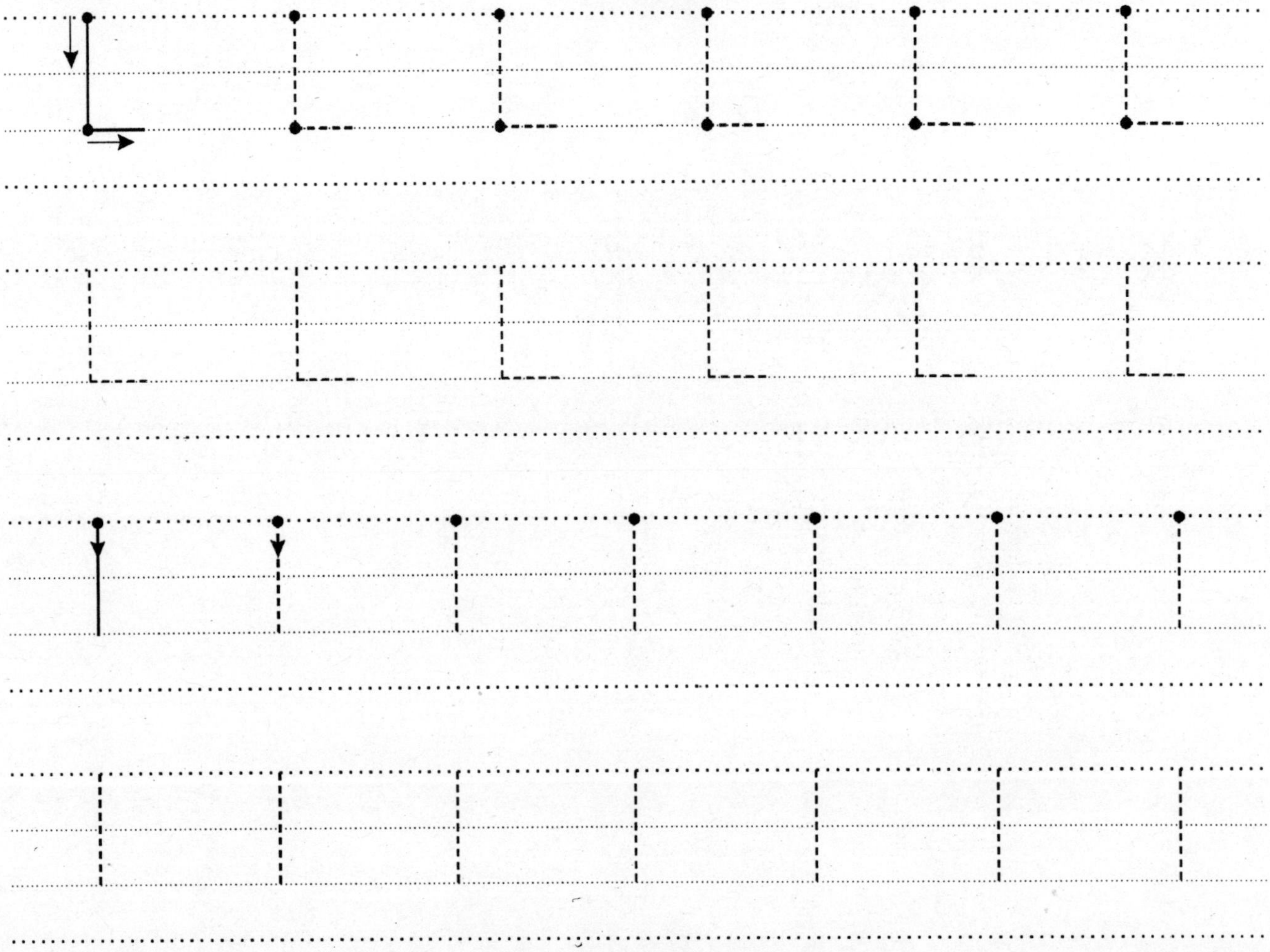

Teacher/Parents : Help the child to complete the letter. Ask him to read aloud and identify.

Alphabet

Trace the letter **M m**.

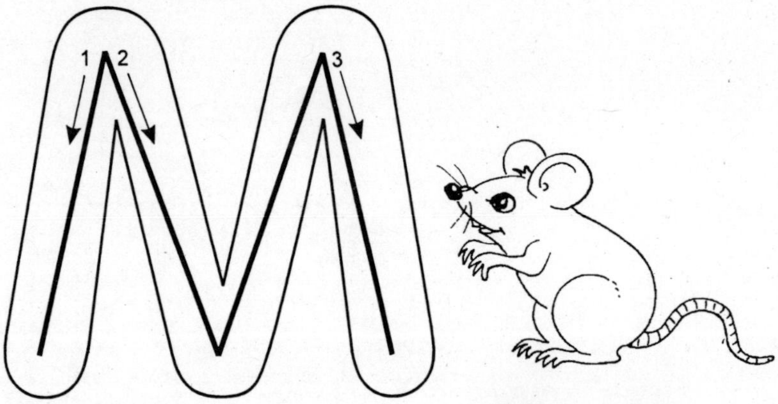

Mouse

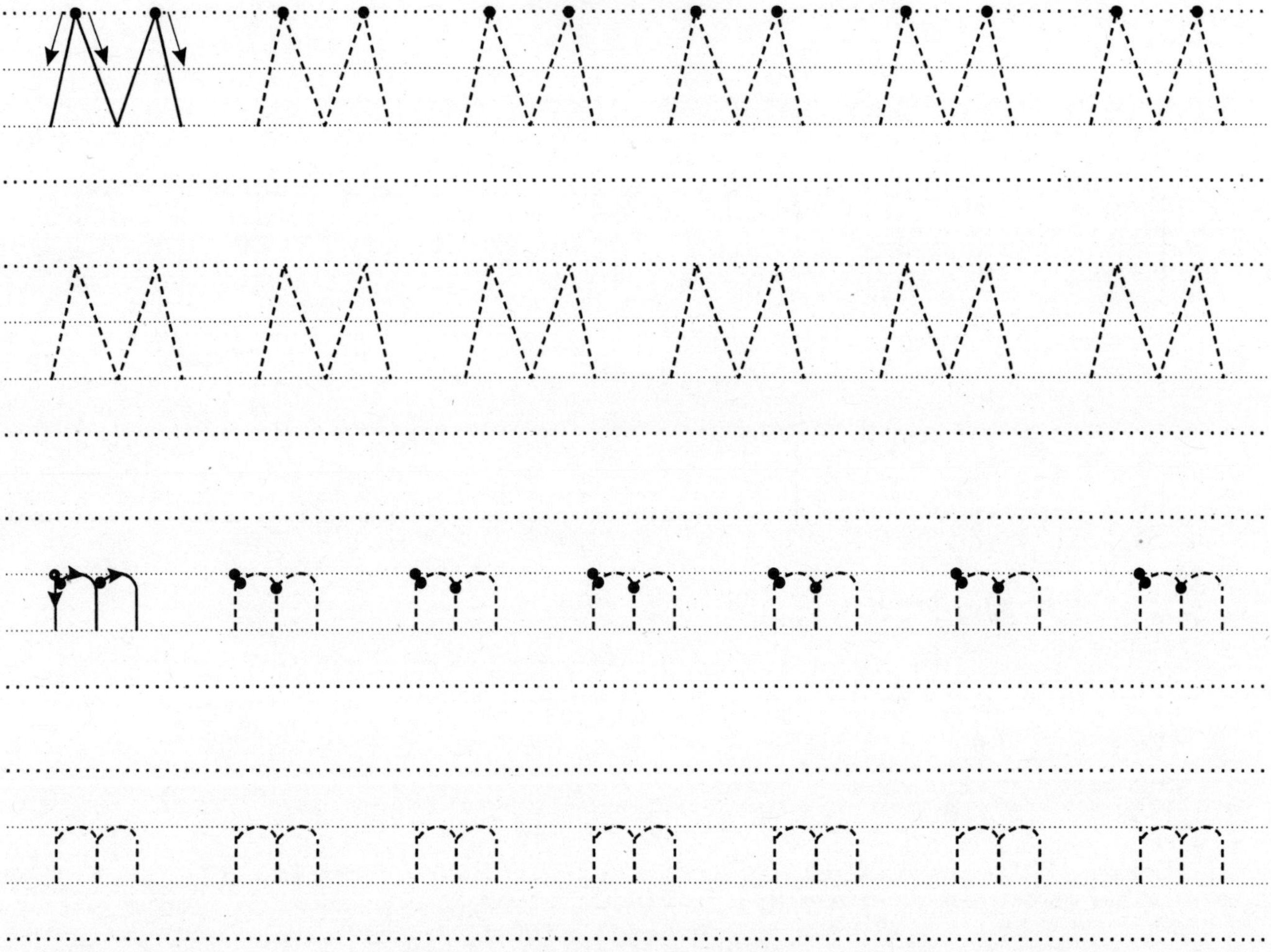

Teacher/Parents : Ask the child to read and identify the letter.

Alphabet

Trace the letter **N n**.

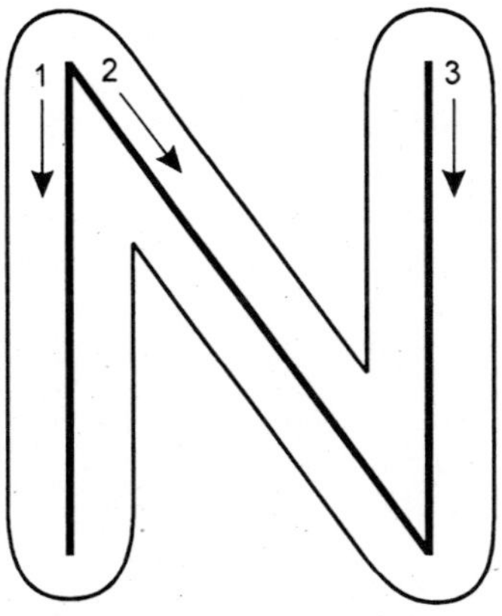

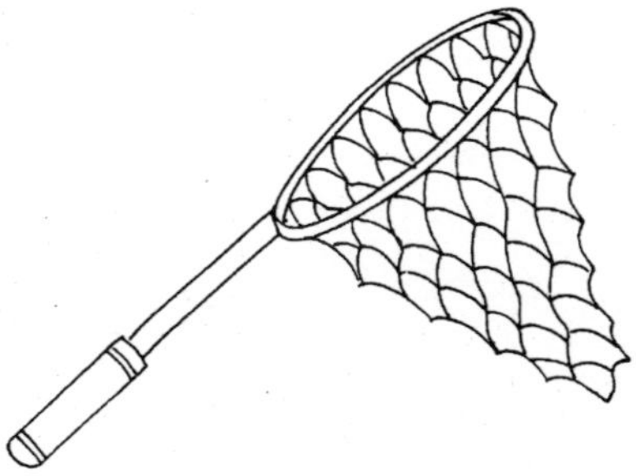

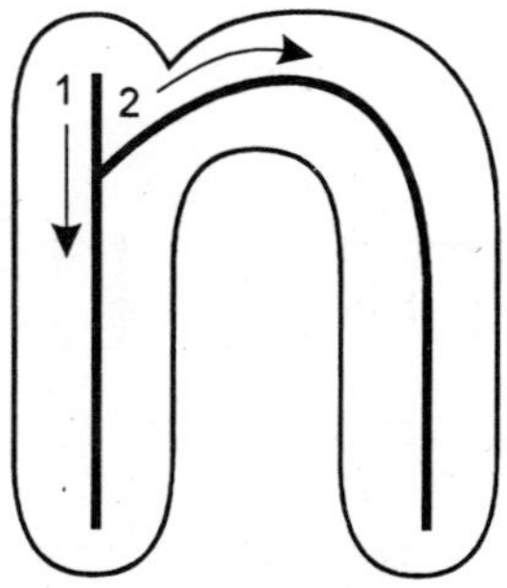

Net

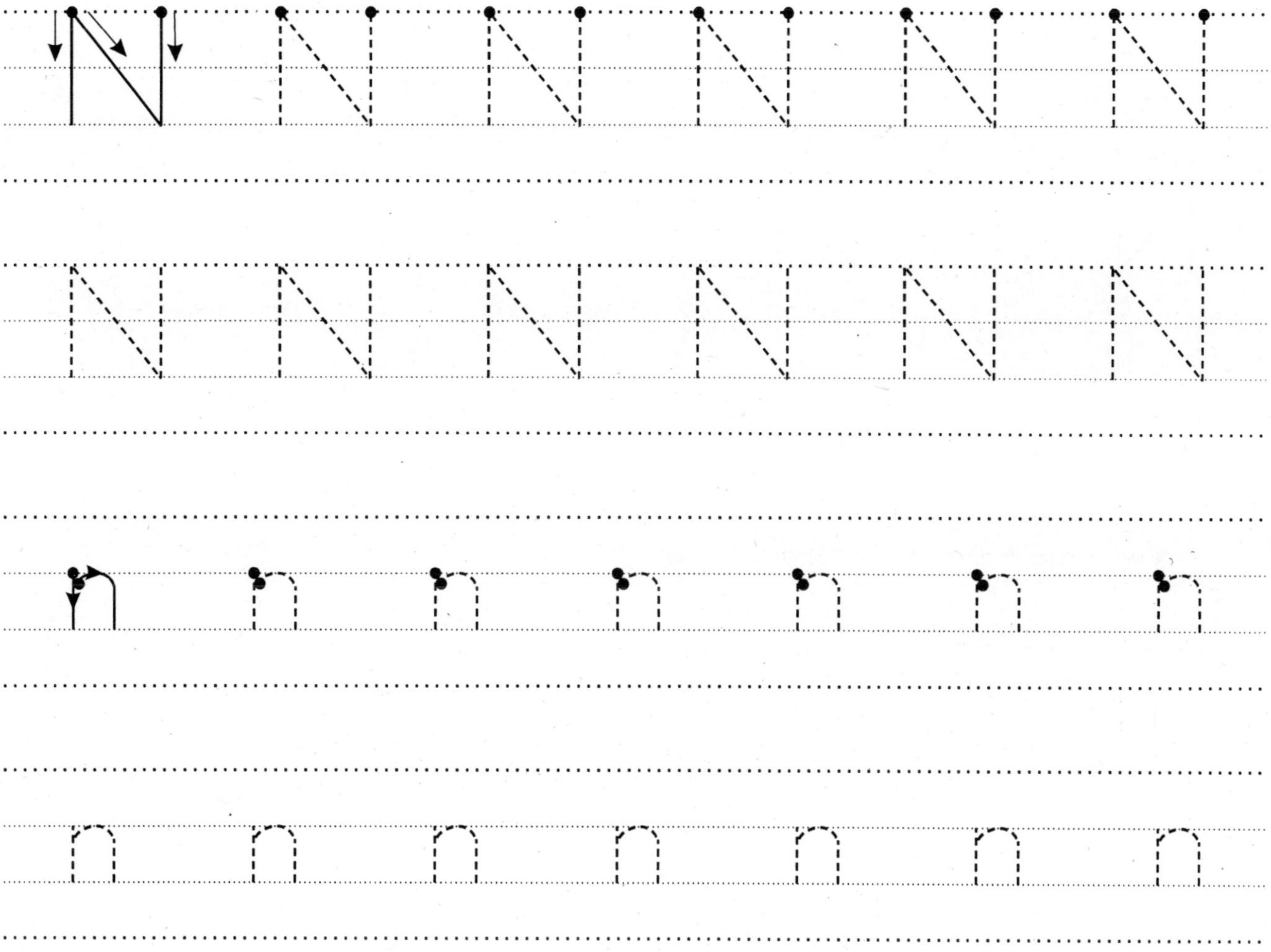

Teacher/Parents : Ask the child to complete the letter shape and identify.

M M M M

M

m m m m m

m

N N N N

N

n n n n n

n

Trace the letter **O o**.

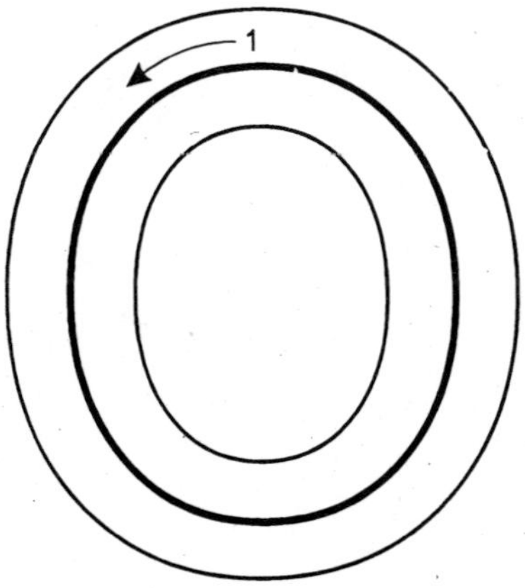

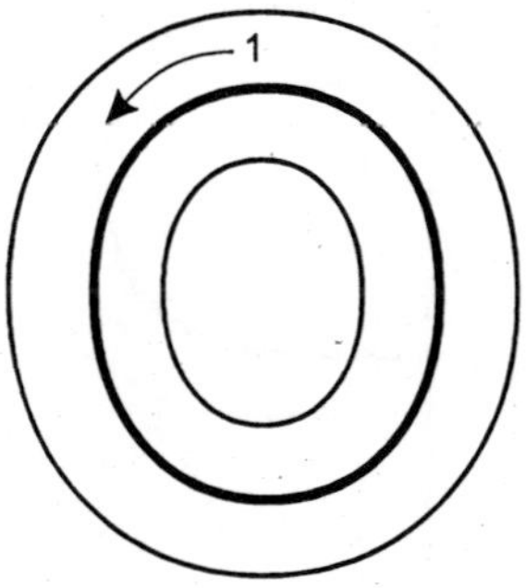

Ox

Teacher/Parents : Ask the child to complete the letter and read aloud.

Alphabet

Trace the letter **P p**.

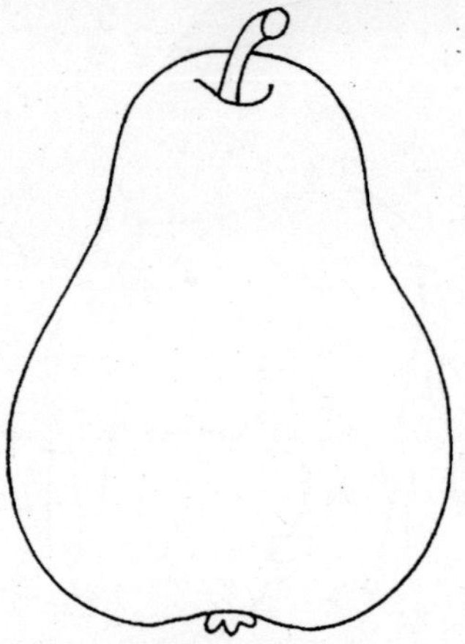

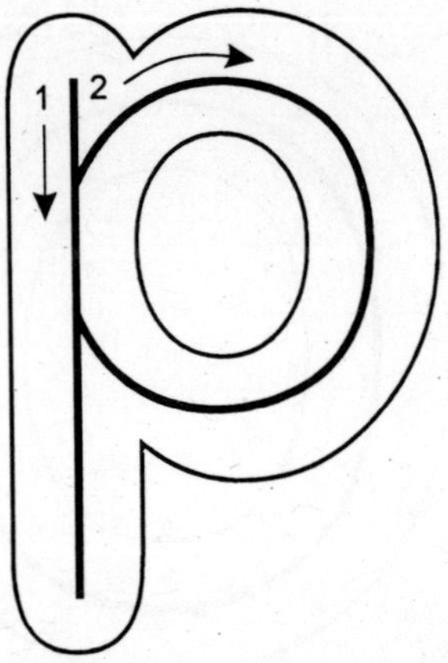

Pear

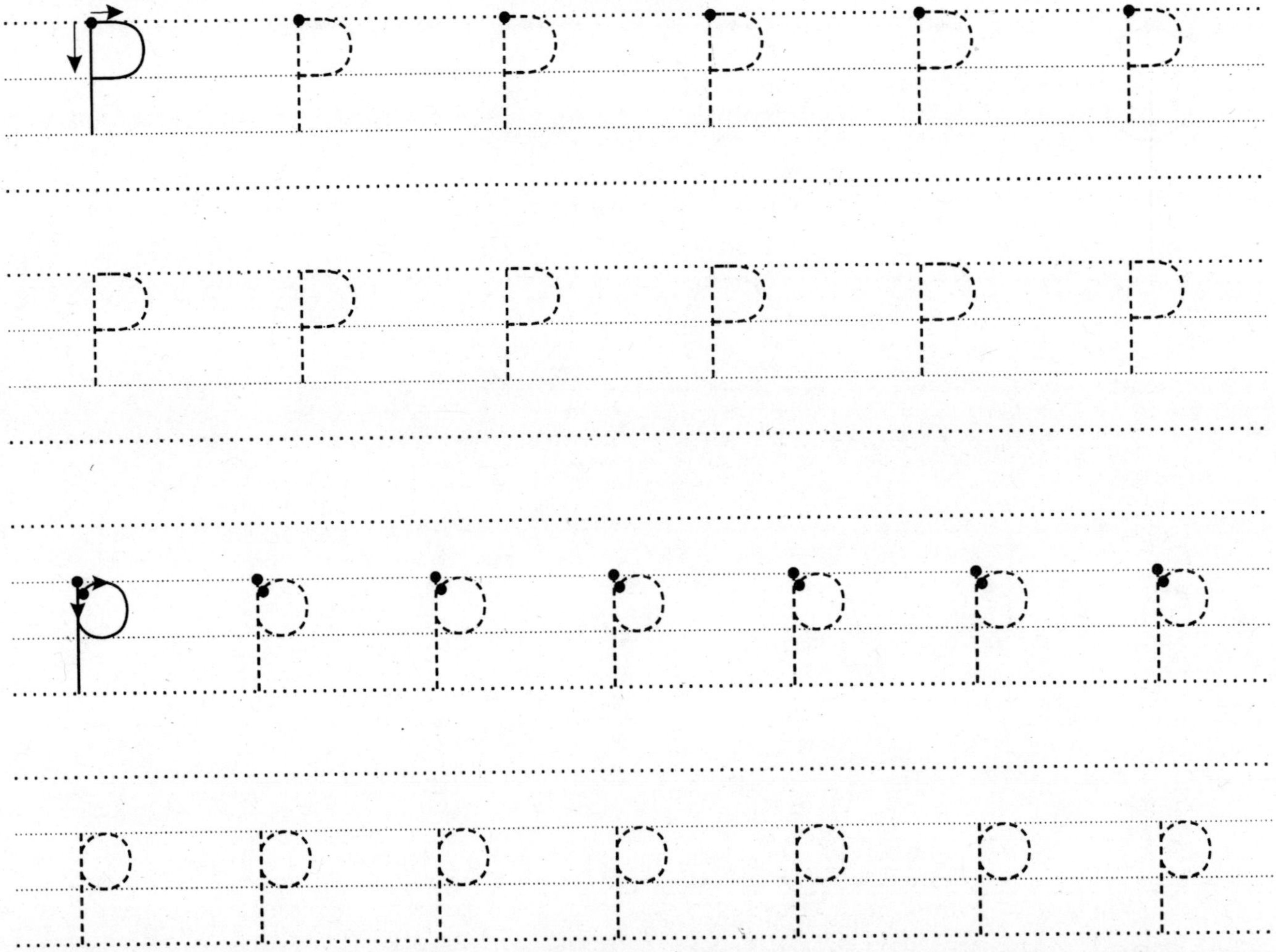

Teacher/Parents : Help the child to complete the letter. Ask him to read aloud and identify.

O O O O

O

o o o o o

o

P P P P

P

p p p p p p

p

Alphabet

Trace the letter **Q q**.

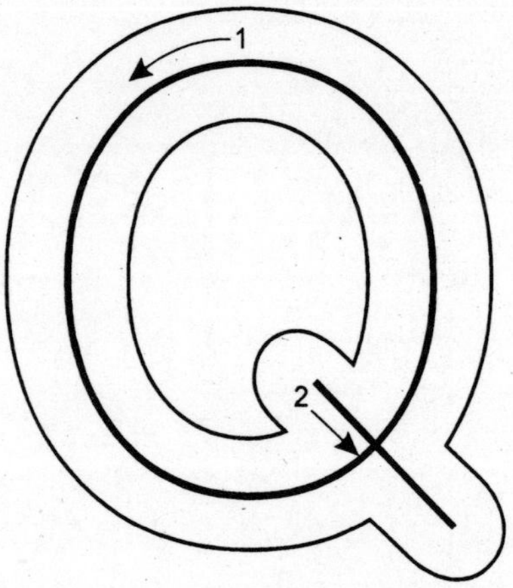

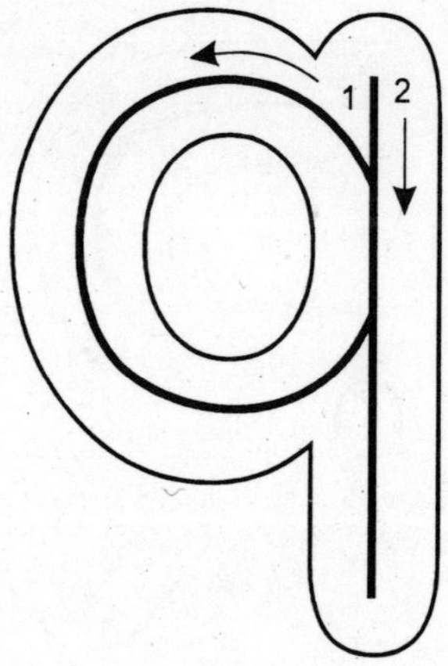

Queen

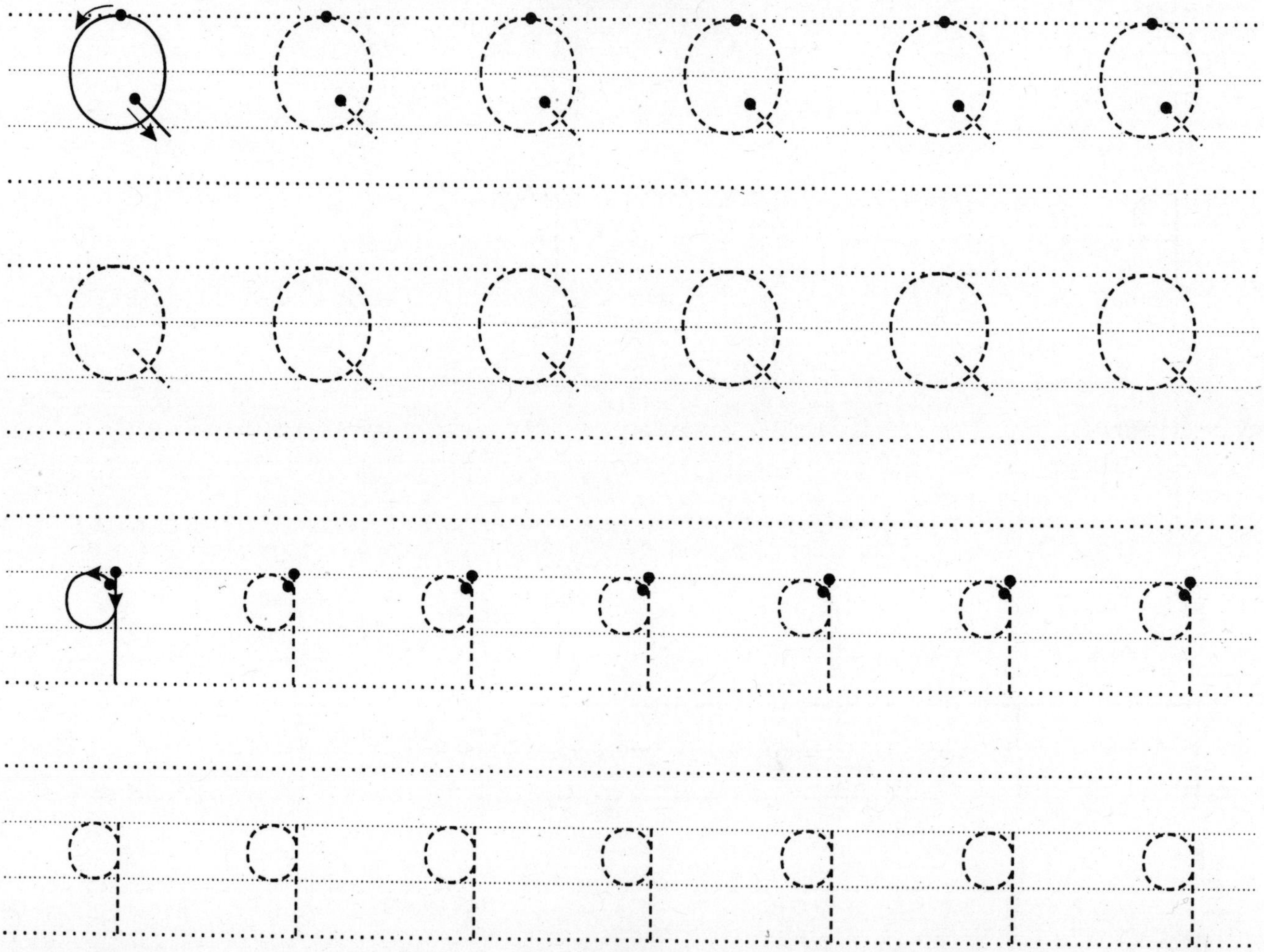

Teacher/Parents : Help the child to join the dots. Ask him to read aloud and identify the letter.

Trace the letter **R r**.

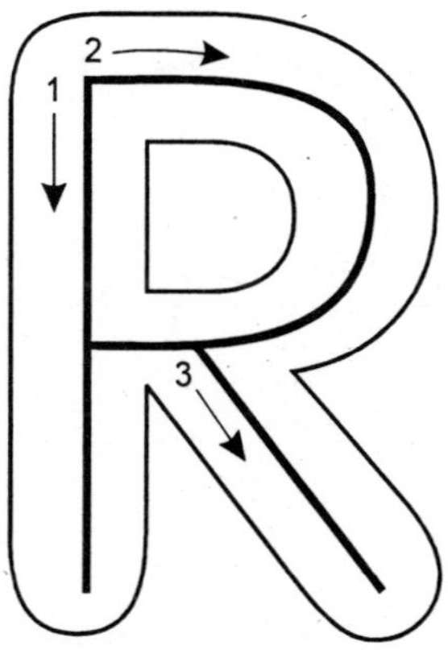

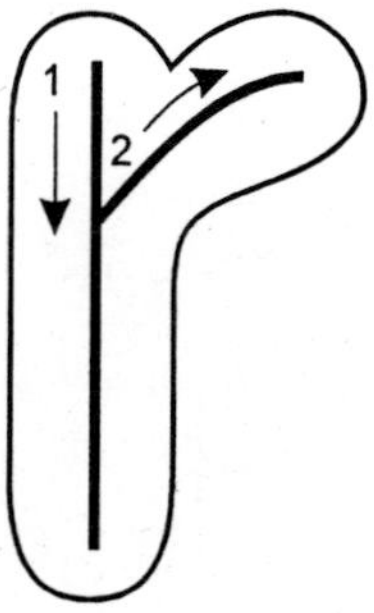

Rose

Teacher/Parents : Help the child to complete the letter. Ask him to read aloud and identify.

Q Q Q Q

Q

q q q q q

q

R R R R

R

r r r r r

r

Alphabet

Trace the letter **S s**.

Sheep

Teacher/Parents : Help the child to complete the letter. Ask him to read aloud and identify.

Trace the letter **T t**.

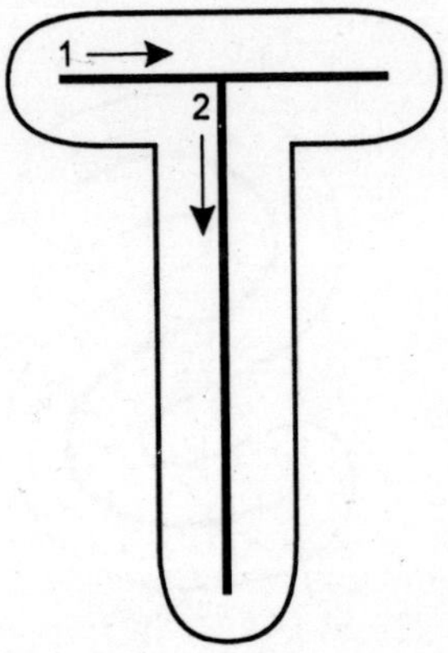

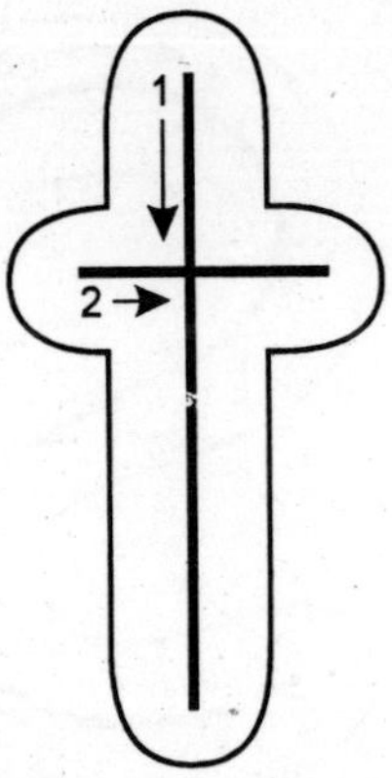

Turtle

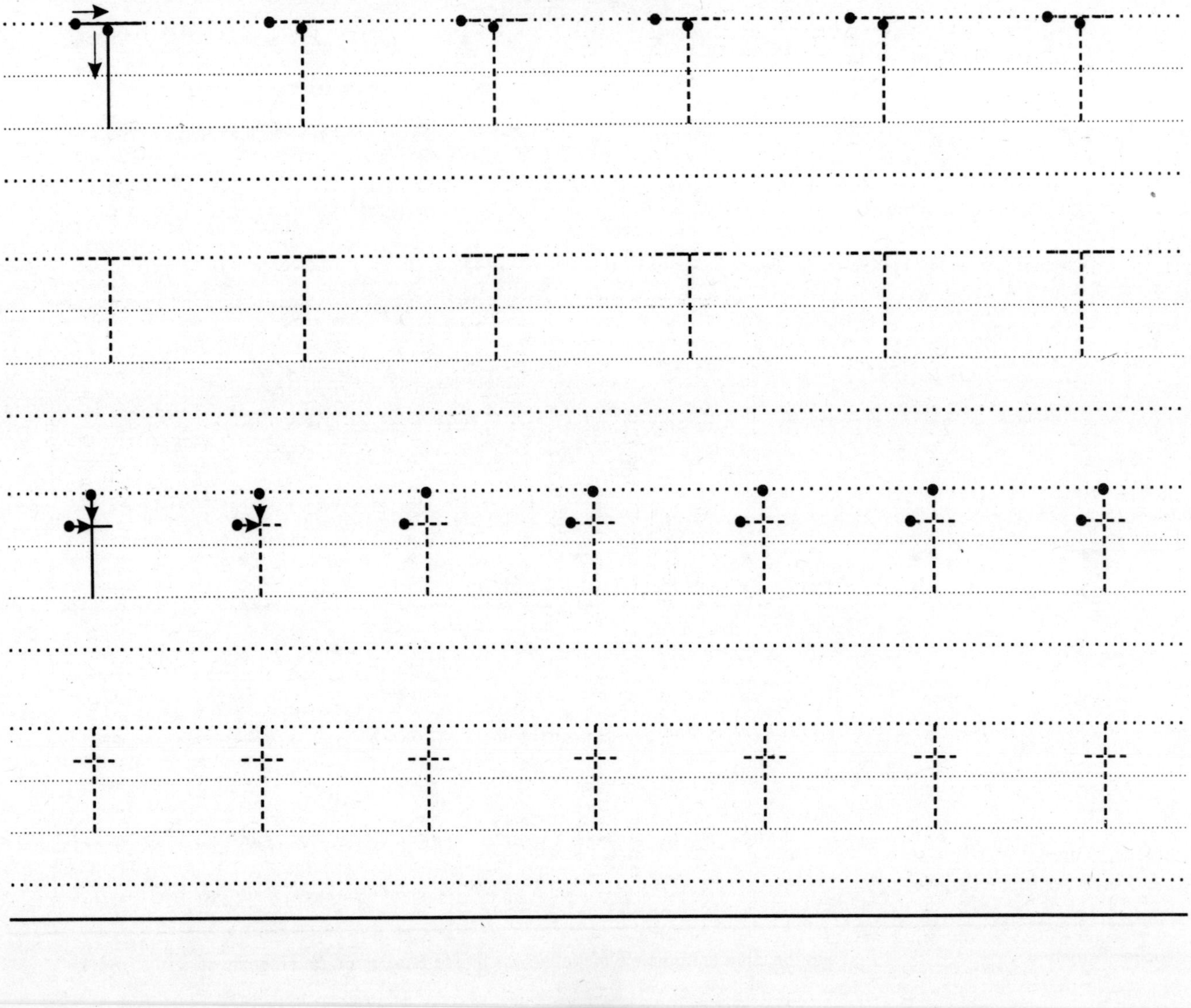

S S S S

S

s s s s s

s

T T T T

T

t t t t t

t

Trace the letter **U u**.

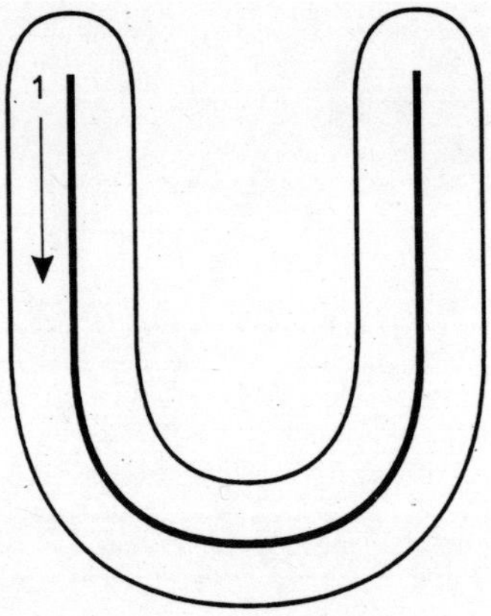

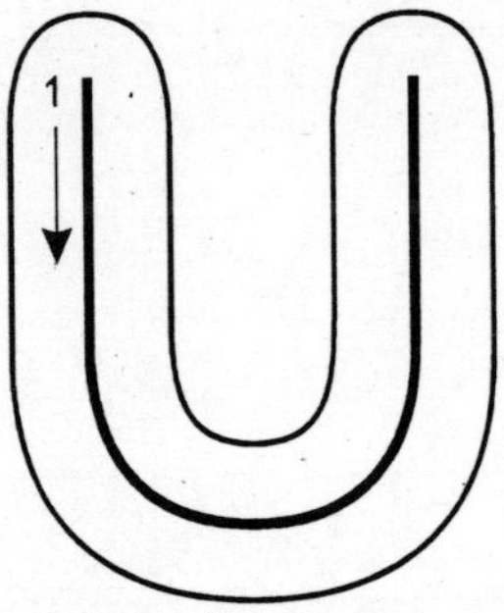

Umbrella

Teacher/Parents : Ask the child to read and identify the letter.

Trace the letter **V v**.

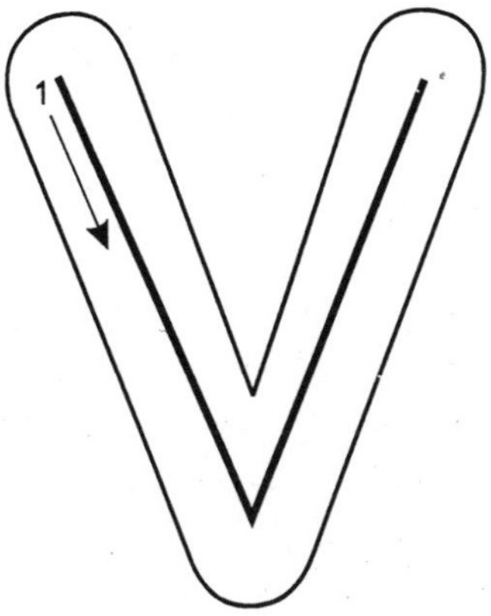

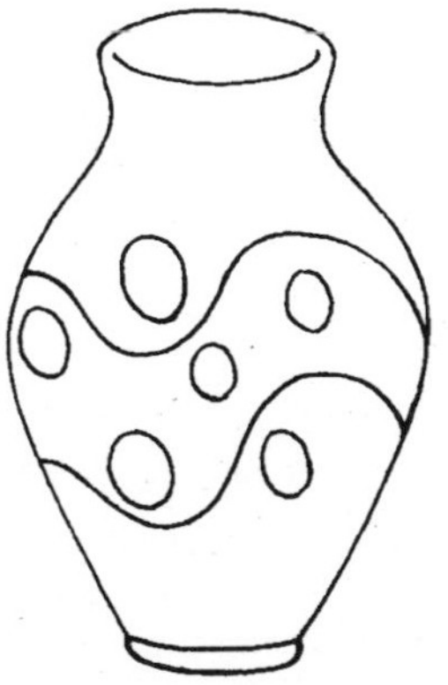

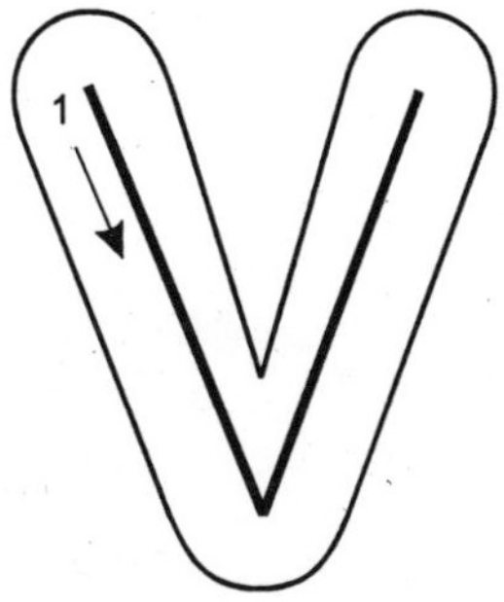

Vase

Teacher/Parents : Ask the child to complete the letter shape and identify.

U U U U

U

u u u u u

u

V V V V

V

v v v v v

v

Trace the letter **W w**.

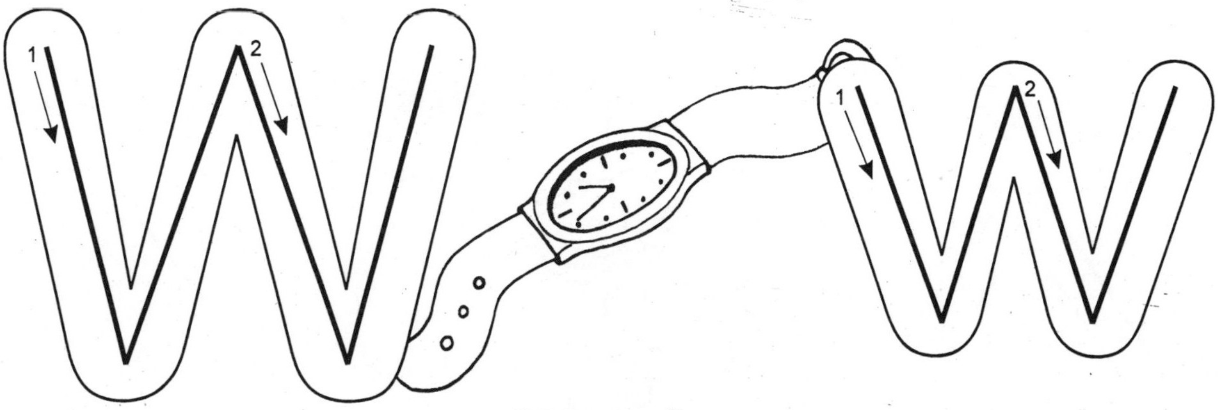

Watch

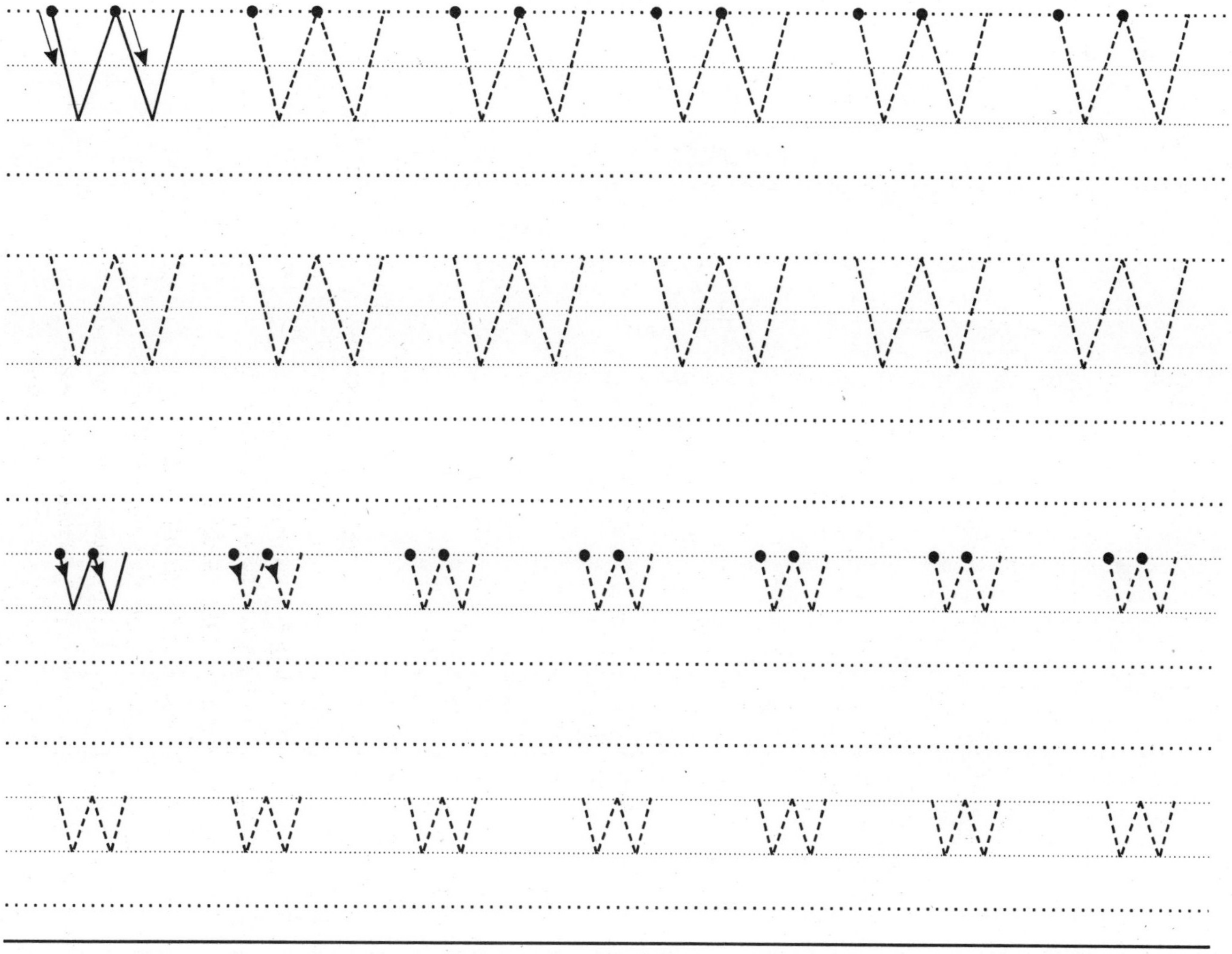

Trace the letter **X x**.

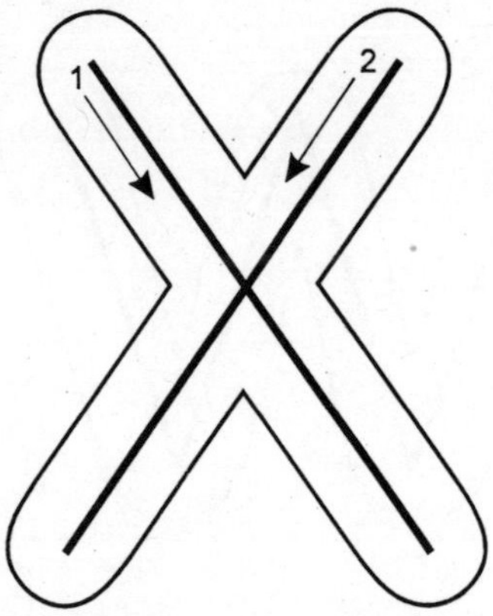

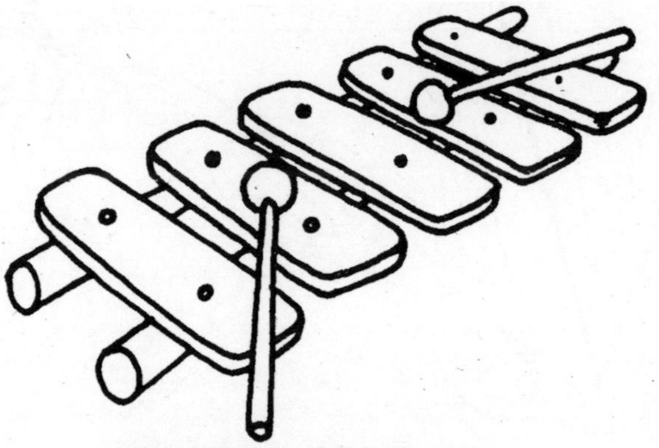

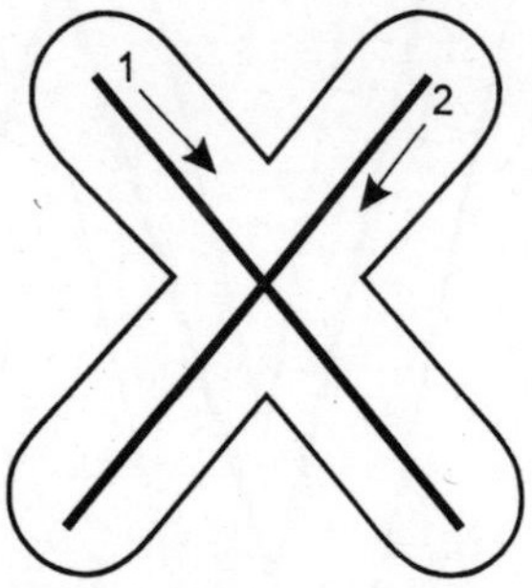

Xylophone

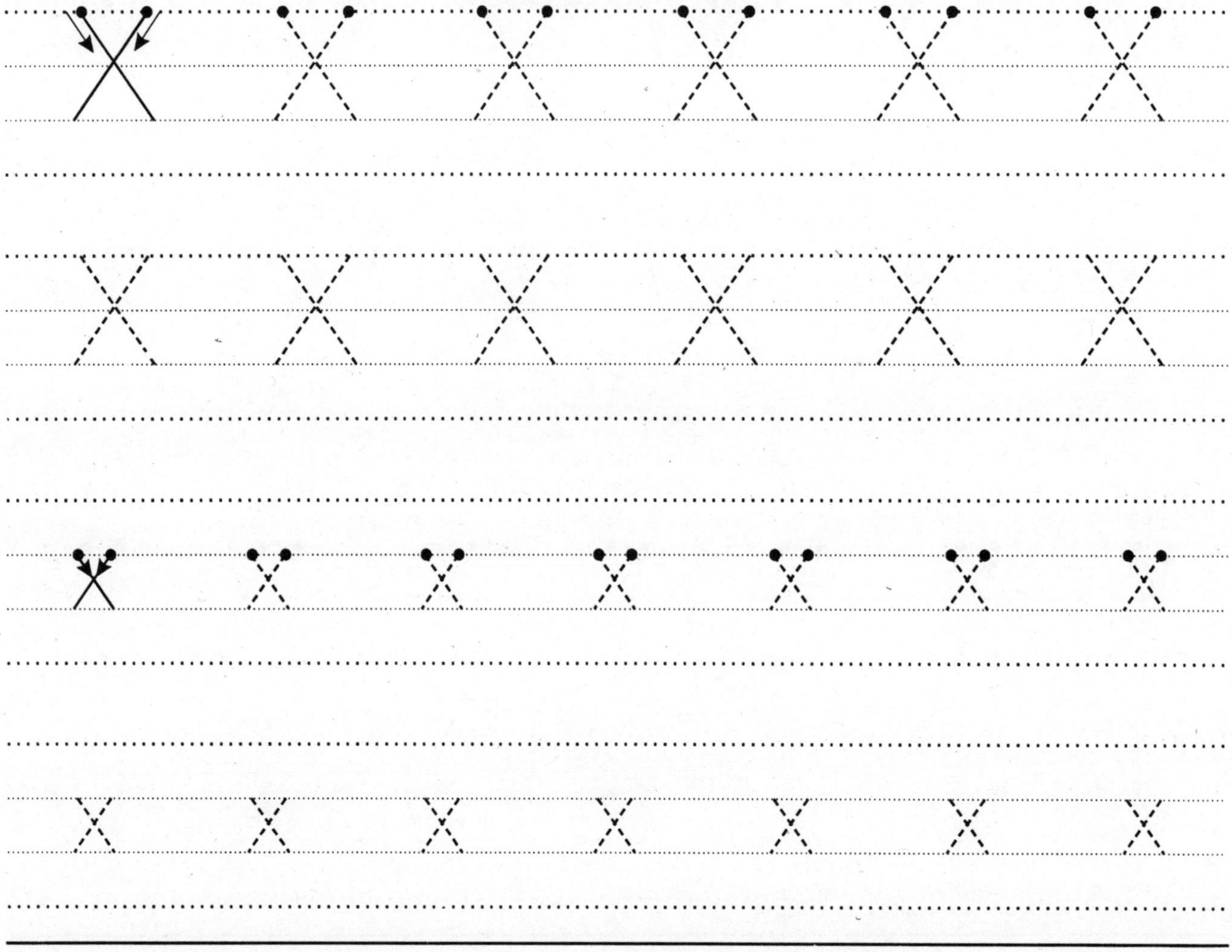

W W W W

W

w w w w w

w

X X X X

X

x x x x x

x

Alphabet

Trace the letter **Y y**.

Yak

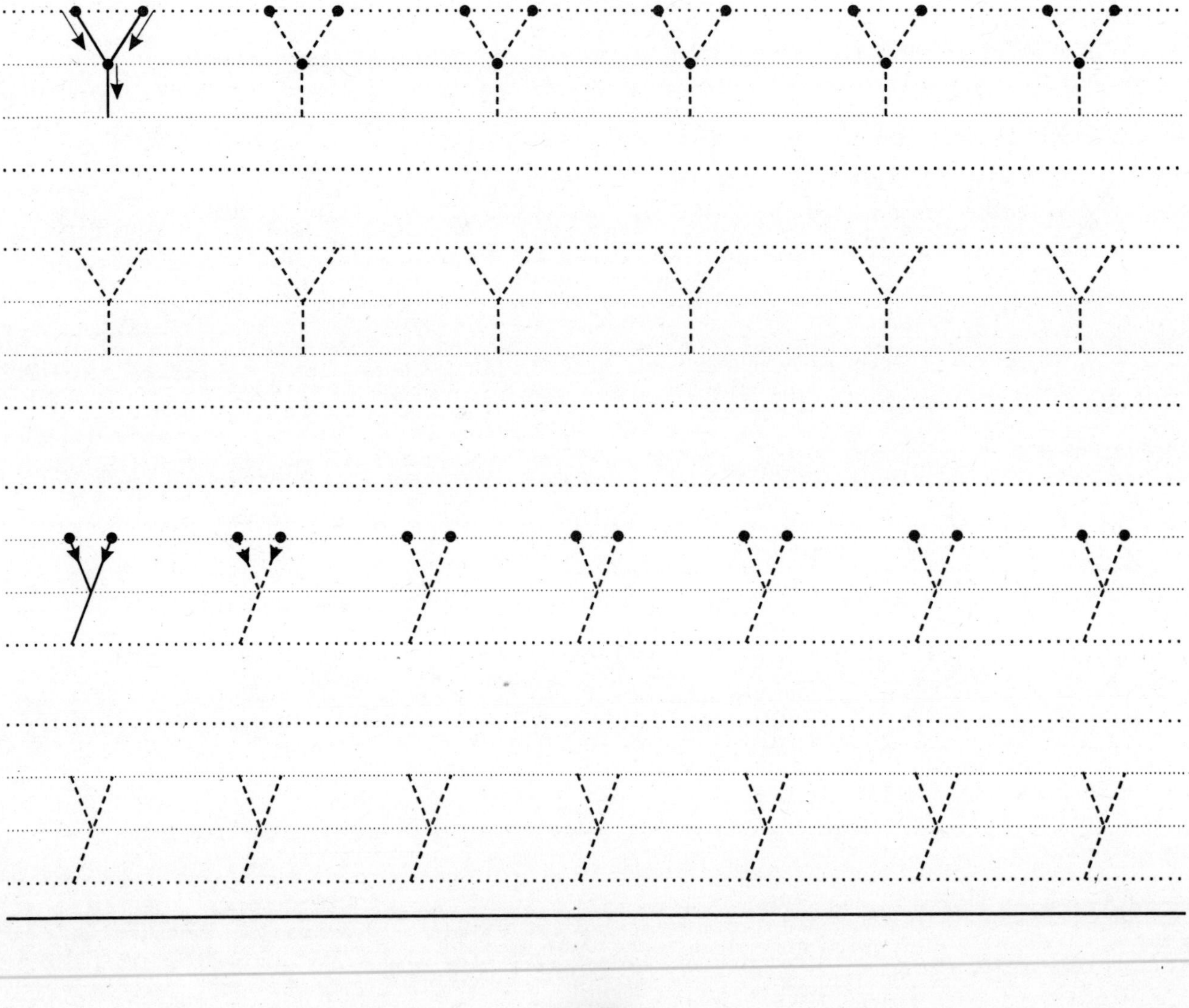

Trace the letter **Z z**.

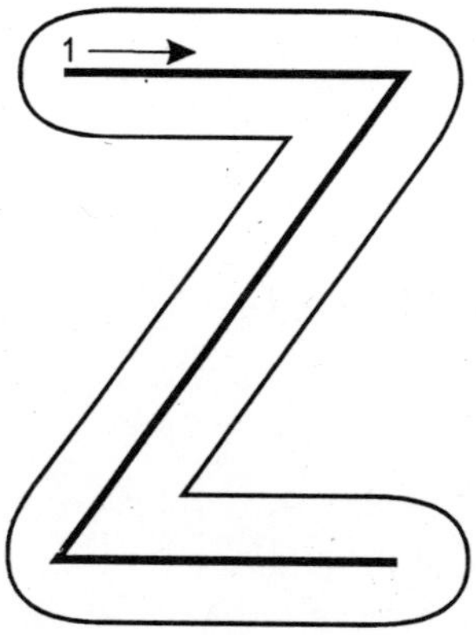

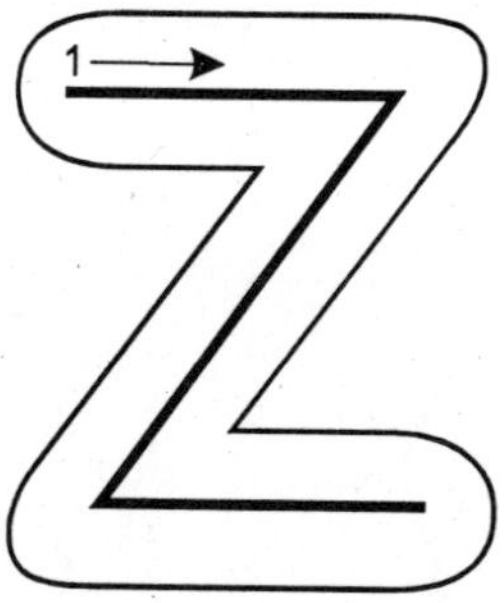

Zebra

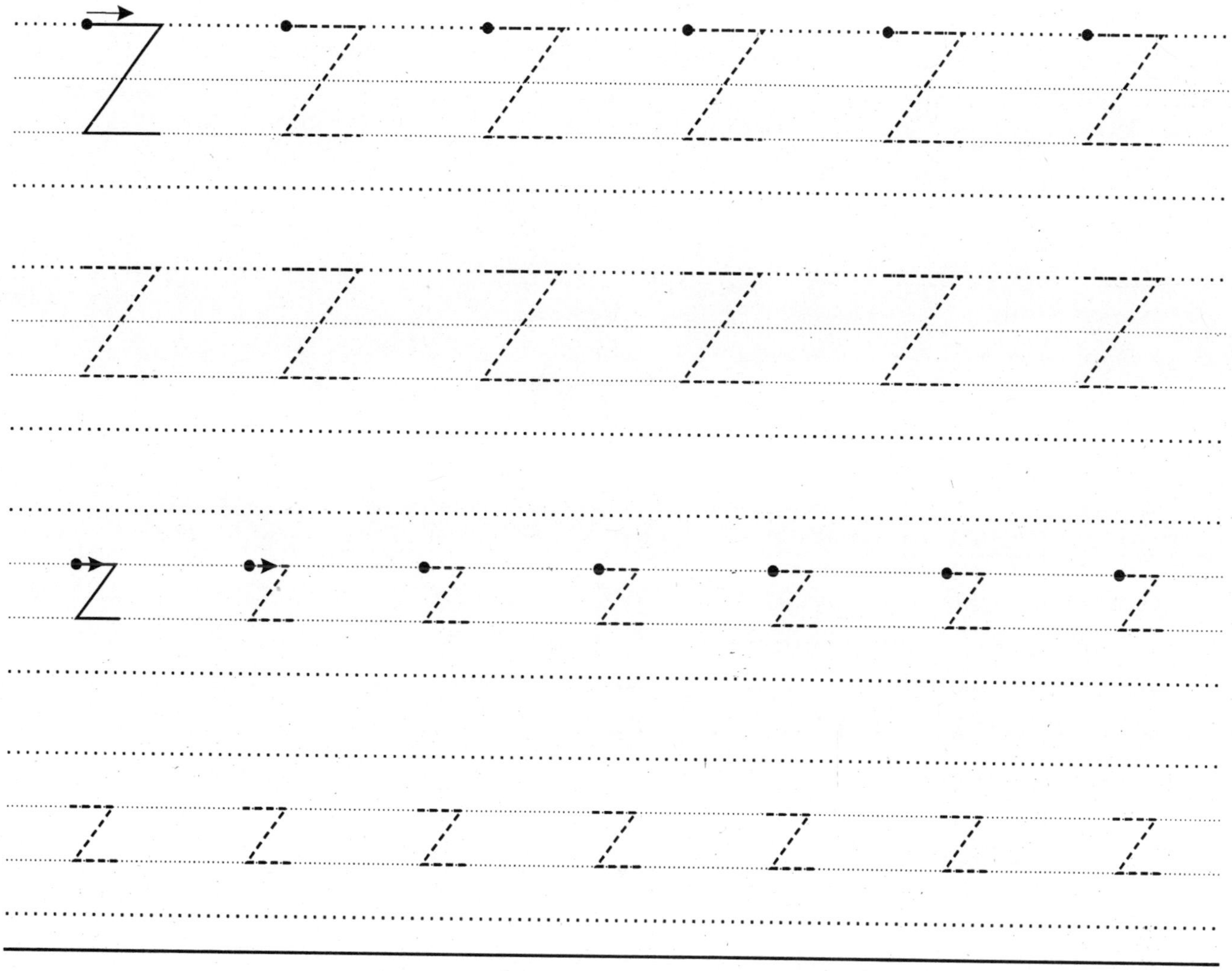

Y Y Y Y

Y

y y y y y

Z Z Z Z

Z

z z z z z

z